MORE Clean Your House & Everything in It

MORE Clean Your House & Everything in It

by Eugenia Chapman
& Jill C. Major

A PERIGEE BOOK

To obtain the best results with maximum safety,
the authors and the publisher recommend
that you read and follow the instructions provided in this
book and listed on the suggested cleaning aids
carefully and entirely *before* beginning any task.

Perigee Books
are published by
The Putnam Publishing Group
200 Madison Avenue
New York, NY 10016

Library of Congress Cataloging in Publication Data

Chapman, Eugenia.
More clean your house & everything in it.

Includes index.
1. Cleaning.   I. Major, Jill C.   II. Title.
III. Title: More clean your house and everything in it.
TX324.C49   1984   648'.5   84-7030
ISBN 0-399-51095-8 (pbk.)

Printed in the United States of America
1 2 3 4 5 6 7 8 9 10

To those people who made this book possible: Ken Major, Senior Partner; Rachelle, Chris, Melanie, Byron, Jason and Cameron, Junior Partners; Donna June Chapla, Manuscript Consultant; B. J. Provost, Child Care Professional; Grandma Jentzsch, Home Beautification Engineer; and Glenna Carter, Home Executive.

CONTENTS

CONTENTS

Introduction: The Cleaning Expert Who Hates to Clean!

Bed maker
Rug shaker
Family waker
Cake baker
Lawn raker
Children taker

HOME MAKER!!
—Jill C. Major

Before you get any further into this book, I want to explain to you one thing: I hate to clean! If you read our first book, *Clean Your House & Everything in It,* then you know that it was written from the perspective of my mother, who is the head housekeeper of the famous Brigham Young Lion House and had her own housecleaning business for thirty years. She is also the proud mother of eleven children and forty-two grandchildren who have given her many opportunities to experiment in cleaning everything from crayon murals on the walls to glue in the carpet. She represents all of you women and men who thrive on glistening windows, waxed floors, and fingerprintless walls.

More Clean Your House & Everything in It is written from my perspective—that of a homemaker who hates to clean but must do it anyway. I am child number seven and I was Mom's greatest challenge when it came to teaching her children to keep a clean house. Often Mom threatened, "If this room isn't spotless, you will not go out on a date tonight!" Of course the room was spotless in minutes, but the closet was filled to overflowing.

Now after ten years of marriage and six children I still struggle with housecleaning. When I get up in the morning I always start with a very simple plan; I either plan to clean or I plan not to. I would much rather read a good book, write, and/or talk on the phone than pick up a broom.

When I see glistening windows I automatically think, "It will rain." When my floors are newly waxed, the thought of twelve muddy feet marches through my mind and to me, spotless walls are nothing but a prime target for a toddler with a magic marker.

LINES TO FOUR SMALL CHILDREN

I often am inclined to think
That it would be much wiser,
To give myself the vitamins
And you the tranquilizer.
—Janet Henry

By now you may be wondering how I got to be a housecleaning expert since I am obviously not overly fond of the subject. Well, it happened this way: Three years ago, on February 18, my sweet sister Carol called from her home in Pocatello, Idaho. "I just had a wonderful idea," she exclaimed. "I've decided that you should help Mom write a book with all of her housekeeping hints in it."

I was cradling my brand-new, fresh-from-the-hospital baby son. My older children were anxiously showing me all that I had missed since I had been away: colorful homemade "get well" cards, the exact spot where Melanie had thrown up, a new face that Grandma Jentzsch had taught them to make by curling over their bottom lip and sticking out their tongue.

I looked at all the confusion and laughed at my sister's "wonderful idea." Later when I called Mom and shared this great joke with her, she listened quietly. Not one giggle escaped her. "It's a good idea," she said. "In fact, I've been thinking that same thing for quite a while."

So we got down to work. We were sure that we could conquer the project in six months. Two years later I had only the first four chapters completed, but that was enough to send to ten major publishers. I wrote a cover letter to assure each publisher that Mom and I could easily complete the book in three months.

Our enthusiasm for the project waned after receiving nine letters that stated, "We are sorry, but we really aren't interested in your book."

When I saw the tenth and last letter in my mailbox, I immediately knew that something exciting was about to happen. Instead of the typed, self-addressed, stamped envelope that I had sent with the first chapters of our book, there was a beautiful white bond envelope, with the Grosset & Dunlap heading on the upper left-hand corner (Grosset & Dunlap was later merged with The Putnam Publishing Group). With trembling hands I ripped open the letter, then I stood by the mailbox and screamed. They wanted to see the entire manuscript as soon as possible!

I immediately called Mom, who was visiting my brother. We were both thrilled until it occurred to us that the Grosset & Dunlap editor was expecting to have a manuscript on her desk in two weeks!

We dropped everything else we were doing. My husband, Ken, took vacation leave from work and Mom and I wrote about housecleaning while he cleaned the house and tended the children. It took two years to complete the first four chapters and two and a half weeks to write the last nine chapters. That has to be a record of some kind.

———————

Nostalgia is like a grammar lesson. You find the present tense and the past perfect.

———————

11

You might think that this was the end of the story, but actually this is where the fun began. After the book came off the press I received a call from Grosset & Dunlap. "A producer from 'Hour Magazine' will be calling you today," the publicity department informed me.

"That's wonderful!" I exclaimed. "What is 'Hour Magazine'?"

With three preschoolers I find my daytime TV watching usually limited to children's programming. My favorite actor is Big Bird. I had no idea that "Hour Magazine" was televised in more than 130 markets to millions of people.

A few weeks later we passed through that invisible barrier that separates "plain folks" from those unique people that glow with Hollywood stardust when we drove a rented Ford into the guarded parking lot of a Hollywood TV studio and squeezed it in between a limousine and a Cadillac. I felt like Cinderella arriving at the ball in a seedy carved pumpkin instead of the golden coach her fairy godmother had promised her.

We were quickly escorted to our dressing rooms, where our names were printed in gold script on long cards which slid neatly into a slot at the top of each door. They were right next door to Michael Landon's dressing room. Landon was also filming a segment for "Hour Magazine" that afternoon. Little Joe Cartright looks quite different with his bushy head of graying hair.

First there was a trip to the makeup room, where a couple of artists sculpted two plain-looking housewives into two plain-looking housewives with a lot of makeup on. Then we were led into the greenroom (which was not green), where a rich buffet meal was spread out for the show guests and staff.

It was fascinating to see the number of people it took to run a TV show. There was one person with a plug sticking out of his ear whose sole job was to make sure we never got lost. Every time we walked out of a room he would smile and give us clearance.

Just before we went onstage another staff member tapped on our dressing room door. "Sign these, please," he said.

"What are they?" we inquired.

"Union papers. You have to belong to the actors' union before we can pay you," he answered.

I can see now why those poor actors went out on strike. Their minimum wage is only about $75 a minute. Who could possibly live on that?

Finally we were escorted down to the stage. The first thing we noticed was that it could use a good cleaning. I had to restrain Mom from taking out her scrub bucket and Spic and Span. Just in the nick of time *he* appeared— tall, lean, and handsome Gary Collins. (He wears makeup too.) He stepped to the front of the stage and introduced us. "Today we have with us house-cleaning experts Eugenia Chapman and Jill C. Major."

I wanted to say, "Mom's the expert. I'm just the writer!" But I didn't. Instead for five magical minutes we explained to him how to use catsup to polish copper, Worcestershire sauce to polish brass, lemon oil furniture polish to clean the shower, Coke to remove stains in the toilet, and so on. When we got down to the club soda, Mr. Collins said, "At my house I use this to take stains off of my carpet. What do you use it for?"

I was stunned. I couldn't imagine Gary Collins bent down over a dirty carpet with a rag in hand. He surely brought home much more than the minimum wage we poor actors' union members were making. He could afford a maid.

I boldly challenged him. "I don't believe it. Do you really help clean your house?"

He stopped for a second and then smiled and assured me, "I don't like to, but yes, I do."

When we left that Hollywood set the stardust went in a hurry. (Mom probably scrubbed hers away. She can't stand dust.) But there were many other opportunities to do radio and TV shows, including a spot on a local TV station that I do solo because of Mom's demanding work and lecture schedule. Each week I am introduced as a "housecleaning expert." Now people stop me in the stores and on the streets calling out, "Hey, housecleaning lady." I know how a doctor feels as I give out free advice every day to people who want to know how to cure their ailing awnings, sick sinks, dying drapes, or the rash in their toilets. Don't get me wrong. I love the attention. In fact I am thrilled from the top of my toilet brush right down to the bottom of my broom. The only problem is that I still hate cleaning!

Don't think of it as dirty. Think of it as earthy.

———————

If you too hate cleaning you belong to an elite group. Some of the great geniuses of our time were sloppy housekeepers. If Sir Alexander Fleming had always washed out his dishes after he used them he would never have discovered penicillin. And that legendary sauce whose name no one can pronounce was a result of Lea and Perrin not discarding their rotten-tasting experiments for months at a time. This natural aging process turned out to be the secret of Worcestershire sauce.

Who knows, that stack of dishes in the sink, moldy delicacies in the refrigerator, or bottles on the shelf that are turning brown with age just might be the start of something big.

If you have discovered that the eleventh commandment is not "Cleanliness is next to godliness" (that saying isn't even in the Bible), I promise that this book will give you the knowledge you need to do as much cleaning as you want and never make you feel guilty about what you leave undone. If you are like my mother and really love to clean house, then there are many new ways in this book to track down dirt and destroy it. Either way, relax and have fun because that's what I'm going to be doing.

———————

Whoever said, "A job well done never needs doing over" obviously never spent much time doing housework.

———————

14

1 Family Planning

Anybody who isn't pulling his weight is probably pushing his luck.
—Franklin Jones

One thing that generally happens when a book comes out is that it is reviewed by critics from magazines and newspapers. *Clean Your House & Everything in It* received great reviews. In fact, it received only one real criticism and this was from a *Washington Post* writer. Her gripe was that "Eugenia Chapman and Jill Major still think of cleaning as women's work . . . they refer to the housecleaner as 'she' and 'her.'" The critic then goes on to say, "If you can get past this unfortunate viewpoint . . . both men and women should benefit from some of the tips the authors provide."

In answer to this let me quote some statistics from the American Home Economics Association. They report that men married to homemakers spend six minutes per day in the kitchen; men with employed wives spend twelve minutes. Women who are employed spend just under five hours on house and family work. Men, whether their wives are homemakers or employed, spend about an hour and a half a day on house and family work. Children spend about as much time on housework as the men do. This means that on the average, husbands and children split 30 percent of the housework while wives do the remaining 70 percent of it.

We would rather not think of housecleaning as women's work. In fact, we would be more than willing to share the fun and joy of cleaning the toilet with not only the man of the house but the children also. But the question is, How do you get the rest of the family excited about this cleaning liberation?

It used to be: A man works from sun to sun but a woman's work is never done.   **15**

Then it was: A woman works from sun to sun, but at five o'clock a man's work is done.

Now it is: No more working from sun to sun. I want some help to get this work done!
—Jill C. Major

———

There has been a lot of publicity about housewives going on strike. A woman from Texas did this for three months. She had been threatening her family for some time that if they didn't start picking up after themselves she would strike. Then one Halloween night there were towels and clothes flung all over the bathroom and that was the explosion point. "I'm their Mother and not their maid," she insisted. The sign across the house read *Mom on Strike—Pick Up or Pack Up.*

I thought seriously about going on strike as I pulled myself out of bed one morning to fix breakfast. Dishes have always been a hassle in our family, as they are in most families, and I had spent long hours trying to teach my children how to do an efficient job. It was the dirt and crumbs that clung to my bare feet that gave me the first clue that someone had missed a lesson in one of my dish-doing classes. I searched for the pot I was going to use to cook cereal in and finally located it in the oven still filled with cold stew. The dishwasher hadn't been turned on the night before and the dishes were coated with a hard crust of brown gravy and dehydrated carrots and onions.

I felt like screaming, "I'm going on strike!"

As I began contemplating the result of this action a vision opened before my eyes:

"Hey, everyone, Mom's going on strike!" The news quickly spread through the family.

While I was painting my signs I heard arguing in the kitchen.

Emerging from strike headquarters, I asked, "What's going on up

here?"

"Don't worry, Mom. We were trying to decide what to have for breakfast. Byron and Jason wanted brownies and Kool-Aid. I voted for pizza. Melanie wanted root beer floats and Chris thought potato chips sounded good. It's all settled now, though. We're going to have all of them. Have a seat. It's almost ready."

I held my queasy stomach and ran outside. Sitting on the damp lawn holding my signs was really boring, so I was glad when the phone rang. Media coverage is everything to a real strike, so I ran inside hoping that it was a news reporter. I stepped on a brownie as I entered the kitchen and it squished between my bare toes. There were pots, pans, and plates stacked to the ceiling and the baby was sitting on the floor in the middle of a pond of Kool-Aid.

"Hello," I answered hopefully.

"Hi, sweetheart. How's the strike going?" my husband asked sweetly.

"Where are you?" I demanded. "You need to be here taking care of the house and the kids while I'm striking."

"Oh, well, that's what I'm calling about. I'm real proud of you for standing up for your rights. In fact, I've decided to follow your example. I'm going on strike too. The guys at work have an extra ticket for the basketball game tonight and . . ."

I waded through a pile of dirty clothes to find the door again. When I opened it there they were—cameras, reporters, and photographers. I put on my best media smile and marched outside, but they weren't the least bit interested in me. Their attention was focused on my six children, who were carrying signs and marching around in a circle chanting, "On strike! On strike!"

Instead of my demands the signs read, *More desserts—No more dishes* and *More allowance—No more piano lessons* and *More TV time—No more baths!*

Then my baby crawled by wearing one of those saggy, baggy diapers. He was carrying a sign in his teeth which read, *More love—No more striking!*

As the vision closed, my eyes opened. The crumbs were still on the floor and the cold stew was in the pan—*what a relief!*

The biggest family problems are those caused by know-it-all kids and yes-it-all parents.

No, striking isn't the answer. Instead we need to take the *Washington Post*'s suggestion and stop thinking of housecleaning as a women's activity. Housecleaning needs to be a family activity, which requires family communication. In our family we initiated a monthly family council. On the first Monday of each month we gather around the negotiating table (located conveniently in the kitchen) and work out the household hassles.

Dishes are one of our biggest problems. Here is an example of the negotiation process that our family has been through over this dilemma:

Problem: Mother is sick and tired of doing breakfast, lunch, and dinner dishes every day.

Solution: The older children, who were then six, seven, and ten years young, got the opportunity to help. ("Who, us?" they screeched. "No," I tell them. "Just the ones who eat and therefore help to dirty the dishes.") They agreed to work together and get the dishes done really fast.

Problem: The children have never learned to cooperate. They fight and argue and it takes forever to get the dishes done.

Solution: Each child is given a specific area of responsibility; for example, one child does the pots and pans; another sweeps the floor, clears off the table, and washes off the counters and stove; another empties the dishwasher; and so on.

Problem: Two years went by and our children started becoming heavily involved in outside activities, so when someone had to leave right after dinner the other children felt picked on because they had to do the escapee's chores.

18   **Solution:** The children each picked two nights that they were not involved

in something and those were their dish nights. On Sundays we all worked together putting the meal on and doing the dishes.

Problem: Wednesday nights everyone had an activity and dishes were not getting done until 9 P.M.—that is, everyone had an activity except Dad. ("Me do dishes?" he exclaimed. "Only if you eat and help dirty the dishes," the family chimed in.)

There is nothing like a dish towel to wipe that contented look off a married man's face.
—Glenn Preston Burns

The evolution of dishwashing responsibility is far from over. We have younger children who will soon be at the age when they too can have the opportunity to help out, and our older children are constantly coming up with new ideas to save time and energy (*their* time and energy, of course). *And* my husband is talking about going back to school, so the negotiations will continue.

If a spouse's words are sharp, maybe it's from trying to get them in edgewise.

During family council we have tried to find solutions to every mundane task that drives us crazy. A problem that bothered my husband was that I never had dinner on the table when he got home, the way his mother always did. It makes sense, since the rest of the evening is free to relax in or do other things if dinner and dishes are over early. My side is valid too. I work just as hard as he does. By the time 5:00 P.M. comes I'm tired and don't feel like hassling over dinner right then. I resented having him come home and read the newspaper while I slaved in the kitchen.

We finally worked out some simple compromises. Once a week, on Ken's day off, he takes over the meal preparation and I get a vacation from cooking dinner. If I am working on dinner when he comes home, he helps me in the kitchen. If I put dinner on the table just when he walks in the door he rewards me with a half hour after dinner to do anything I want to do without the interference of the kids. I use the time to take piano lessons and practice. (I started using the beginning books with the children and I'm now in the fourth year of developing my musical talent.)

Many a wife has found that hugging her husband is the best way to get around him.

Another problem developed with the children's housework. I would get mad at them if they didn't vacuum the floor when they cleaned their rooms. Another day the floor looked reasonably clean so I didn't insist that they vacuum. The children were confused and I had to police the rooms every day before they went to school, telling them what had to be done. In family council we made a schedule that told exactly what each child was supposed to do in his or her room each day. We have hung the schedule on the refrigerator so that everyone can see it and "I forgot" can no longer be used as an excuse. For example, the chart reads that every day beds have to be made. I suggested that they vacuum on Wednesdays and Saturdays. One child raised the objection that Wednesdays were busy for her because of singing lessons. She preferred to vacuum on Tuesdays. That was put on the schedule. The children agreed to dust on Mondays, Wednesdays, and Saturdays. Closets and drawers also had to be straightened on Saturdays (they moaned a lot, but Mom and Dad overruled all the objections).

Adolescence is a period of rapid changes. Between the ages of twelve and seventeen, for example, a parent ages as much as twenty years.

The children also have a room in the house to clean daily and, again, the work is broken down so that they know exactly what has to be done in that room each day. If the work is not completed, the children punish themselves because they are not allowed any "privileges" such as TV until they take care of their responsibilities. Some of our children have chosen to do their work just before bed, so that the early morning schedule isn't so crunched.

_____

A word of praise for neatness and cleanliness is far more satisfactory and
rewarding to the child and to the parents than a scolding.
—Veda Jentszch (my grandmother)

_____

The point is not to copy our compromises and negotiations, because what worked to resolve our conflicts probably wouldn't work for you. The point is to get together and talk about the problems and work out your own solutions.

If you are just beginners at family council meetings (and if you want to avoid making them meetings of the "bored"), here are a few suggestions:

1. Tackle only one or two problems in a session. Working on too many problems at once creates confusion and often resentment.

2. Try to keep the sessions down to about a half hour. We have found for our young family that the children get bored beyond this point. When ennui sets in they fuss and fidget, we get impatient, and the family council is a disaster.

3. Do not point the finger. Instead of saying, "We are sick and tired of the way Johnny keeps his bedroom," discuss the rules and standards that should be met for keeping bedrooms clean.

4. Recognize that this is a family discussion and that children have the right to point out problems that parents are causing. My husband and I have a bad habit of reading the newspaper in the living room and leaving it. When one of the children brought this up in family council we had to agree that it

21

wasn't fair to the person assigned to clean that room. It wasn't easy to admit that, but it made it easier on the children to know that they weren't the only ones who had to change.

The faults of others are like headlights on an automobile. They always seem more glaring than our own.

---

5. Keep your cool. Family council should be a good experience. If the parents are yelling at the kids and the kids are communicating in a similar way, the result will be bad feelings.

6. Plan a dessert and a game afterward, so that the children and the adults will look forward to family council meetings.

Wife to husband: "I hope you don't have any plans for the rest of the day. I want you to help me for a minute."
—Ed Reed

---

2 Pregnancy & the New Baby

To make your family last, put them first.

I love being pregnant! From the moment that my blossoming belly becomes public property that everyone from my Great-Aunt Mabel to the stranger on the street feels compelled to pat, to that last second when, while I am checking out at the grocery store, my water breaks, I think being pregnant is great!

Whenever I express this feeling to other women, they accuse me of either being crazy or just plain forgetful. With six children I admit that I could be a little on the crazy side, but I definitely haven't forgotten what it is like to be pregnant. Just a little over a year ago I was sitting under this typewriter with my belly button touching the table even though I was an arm's length away.

Twins: wombmates

Now, I will admit that there are a few negative aspects to pregnancy. I have had some disappointments. When I discovered I was pregnant the first time, I immediately asked the doctor, "What can't I do? Scrub the floors? Lift the iron?" Oh, how modern medical science has retrogressed! In my mother's generation they used to recommend that you "take it easy" and "don't overdo it." Now they actually encourage women to stay active. I have read articles on swimming, yoga, bicycling, jogging, and even doing aerobics during pregnancy, so obviously a little heavy-duty housecleaning isn't going to hurt the normal nine months of girth.

I also looked forward to that "burst of energy just before delivery" that everyone talked about. I had plans to clean my house from top to bottom when it hit. Well, I waited and I waited, but nothing happened. Oh, I was bursting in many places, but I never had any extra energy.

Then there are the "small" discomforts. I have never experienced lying across a camel's hump, but I don't think it could be any more uncomfortable than trying to sleep on a pregnant belly. There is the rolling from side to side, adjusting two or three pillows with each move until finally you are completely exhausted from the effort and sleep comes. An hour later it is time for that nocturnal journey to the john and the process of trying to get comfortable starts all over again.

A queasy stomach is another complaint. My first doctor told me it was all in my head. He just about had it all in his lap!

While we are on the subject, there are also a few other annoyances. Number one on my list is the people who ask, "Haven't you had that baby yet?" And I don't like trying to avoid bumping heads with my belly as I squeeze between two rows at the theater, or wearing those fashionless bell-bottom blouses and stretch-panel wonders.

C-section: labor-saving device.
—Jill C. Major

However, these things all seem trivial when compared to the wonderful moments I have experienced while being pregnant: feeling the first flutter of movement, the first real physical indication that a tiny, fully formed human being depended on me for its nourishment and growth; hearing the baby's heart beating rapidly through a monitor at the doctor's office; enjoying the vigorous stretching, kicking, and burping which continually assured me that the baby was healthy; watching our family grow closer as each one of us included in our circle of love another person whom we didn't even know—yet. To me this all adds up to be a nine-month miracle, and miracles are kind of hard to come by these days. That's why I love being pregnant.

Speeches are like babies—easy to conceive, but hard to deliver.
—Pat O'Malley

Even though pregnant women are generally encouraged to stay active, use good common sense. Stumbling is a problem during the last months. One reason it happens is that you can't see your feet or where you are placing them. Be vigilant in nagging everyone to pick up their clothes, toys, and other miscellaneous debris.

As the uterus grows, the center of gravity shifts forward. There is a curvature of the lower back called "lumbar lordosis" that puts a strain on the posture and may affect the pregnant woman's balance. High places may affect equilibrium and cause dizziness.

That last paragraph sounds academic but I put it here so you can show it to your sweetheart and tell him, "That's why I shouldn't be doing any ladder work." If that doesn't convince him to do it for you, then you can scrub walls and ceilings with a sponge mop. Be sure to put a towel over the mop and wipe the walls dry or they will streak. Use a long-handled squeegee to do high windows. If the squeegee doesn't come with a long pole, put it on the end of your broomstick. De-cobweb high areas by throwing a damp bath towel over a broom.

Overdue: Hanging in there while hanging out there.
—Jill C. Major

Bending over becomes difficult and uncomfortable during the last months. It may be a joy to those who are into touching their toes a hundred times during exercise class, but to those who haven't even seen their toes in months it is an additional chore. I sweep all the objects on the floor into one pile, put a box near the pile and put them in the box all at one time. This way I can sort through the mess at a convenient height.

Purchase a long-handled dustpan to go along with your long-handled broom. To scrub the floor, invest in a good self-wringing mop. Put a dry towel under the mop to wipe the floor dry.

Cleaning the bathtub is one of the worst jobs to do when pregnant. Avoid a bathtub ring by using a water softener such as Calgon in the bath water, or squirt a small amount of liquid dish soap in each bath. A long-handled toilet bowl brush will also help to scrub rings away. Don't scrub showers. Have every member of the family wipe them dry with a squeegee or a towel after each shower and you will never have hard-water stains. To clean the shower, put some lemon oil furniture polish on a rag and rub it on the shower surface, then take a clean rag and wipe it off. *Caution:* Do not put lemon oil on the floor—it's slippery! (To clean hard-water stains, see *Clean Your House & Everything in It,* pages 43-44.)

Housework: labor pain.
—Jill C. Major

The first three months and the last three months, a pregnant woman seems to be tired all the time. Even though this is a normal part of pregnancy, it is very discouraging. Often when you get tired you get grouchy. The things you used to do for your family with a light heart before pregnancy may become drudgery when no part of your expanding body feels light. Get as much help from your family as possible (see Chapter 1, "Family Planning"). Small aids such as having your bed partner help make the bed as soon as you both get up (or better yet, just make it part of his permanent assignment) not only help conserve energy, but they also help your attitude toward your family and your service to them.

The worst time for me is always at dinnertime. That's when I really drag. I try to prepare my meals early in the day and clean up the preparation mess after me. I have gone through four "pregnant summers," and it helps not to heat up the house late in the afternoon. For women who work outside of the home it is easy to throw something into the Crock-Pot before work and have it ready when you get home. Remember that anyone who can read can cook, and this includes schoolchildren, doctors, plumbers, mechanics, carpenters, accountants, and so on.

One Mother's Day I was asked to give a talk in church. I told the congregation that I was going to go home and read the comics while my husband fixed me a baron of beef for dinner. I advised all the mothers to let their husbands do likewise. A young husband took my speech to heart and went home and made dinner for his family. His wife hadn't finished the first page of the newspaper before the call came to rally around the table. When everyone was seated he slid a peanut butter sandwich in front of his wife. She parted the bread and asked, "Where's the beef?"

Keep a supply of disposable plates, cups, and even disposable cookware on hand. Barbecue and picnic outside often. This not only saves on dirty pans, but the floor doesn't have to be swept afterward. Take your spouse out to eat once a week. It is amazing how good even a hamburger tastes when you can walk off and leave the mess for someone else to clean up.

You can be a little more sloppy during pregnancy and it is quite traditionally acceptable. If you don't feel like cleaning, don't. Be sure to take frequent rests with your feet propped up. You not only need them, you deserve them!

Award for delivery: Nobelly Prize.

THE BABY

I remember the first time I took my brand-new baby to church. Just as I walked into the chapel a friend whispered to me, "Your baby spit up." I looked over my shoulder and saw a streak of white rancid-smelling slime running down the back of my dark green dress and dripping on the carpet. Those were the days before I became a housecleaning expert and I had no idea what to do about it. A prenatal baby would never embarrass its mother that way!

To clean up baby's spit-up, sponge the area with a solution of 1 teaspoon of white vinegar to 1 quart of cold water, or 1 teaspoon of baking soda to 1 quart of cold water.

Howling success: The baby who gets picked up.

BABY CLOTHES

Baby clothes can be passed down from generation to generation because they never seem to really wear out. The problem is that they look stained and old because of spit-ups and spills. Using a bib during every meal will save the clothes. I also use a bib with a plastic liner during the drooling stage so that I don't have to change wet tops all day long.

Stained baby clothes should be soaked in cold water before washing. Then wash them in hot water, using bleach (if it is safe for the clothes). If the stain is already set, try the following recipe:

Put into a plastic dishpan ½ cup of powdered dishwashing detergent (or ½ cup Spic and Span or Soilax) and ½ cup of baking soda. Fill the pan with hot water and put in the baby clothes. Swish the clothes up and down about every half hour to forty-five minutes for at least eight hours, then wash the stained clothes in the washing machine.

A perfect example of minority rule is a baby in the house.

BOTTLES

The dishwasher is the greatest invention ever made for cleaning baby bottles. For dishwasherless households, clean bottles in hot soapy water, using a bottle brush. For smells or stains, soak the bottle overnight in hot water with 1 tablespoon of baking soda added. Sour bottles can be prevented if the bottle is rinsed in cold water after each feeding. Sterilize baby bottles and nipples by covering with 2 to 3 inches of water and boiling for five minutes. If you don't like to sterilize bottles, use disposable bottles.

Boil all nipples before using the first time. Since a rubber nipple wears out, always give it a quick safety check before putting it on the bottle. Look for cracking or stickiness and give the nipple a firm tug to make sure it will not pull apart in the baby's mouth.

If the hole in a nipple is too small, place the tip of a toothpick in it until it is a little larger than the size you want and then boil it for five minutes. Let the nipple cool five minutes before removing the toothpick. If the hole is too big then, immediately boil it another five minutes without the toothpick.

Of course all this work can be avoided by breast-feeding. I like nursing because it saves time, money, and bother. I never have to wonder if the bottle is too hot or too cold. And it is impossible to run out of the house and forget the bottle.

Adam and Eve had many advantages, but the principal one was that they escaped teething.
—Mark Twain

CAR SEAT, HIGH CHAIR AND INFANT CARRIER

Wash vinyl, plastic, and chrome parts with 2 tablespoons of Murphy's Oil Soap or Lin-Sol or a few drops of mild liquid dish soap to 1 gallon hot water. Wipe dry.

To remove stains dip a damp cloth in baking soda and scrub.

To brighten the chrome put rubbing alcohol on a rag and rub it on, then wipe it dry.

CLOTH DIAPERS

I estimated that my mother changed over 100,000 diapers for more than twenty-five straight years, and those were the days when men never saw any rear action and mothers laughed at such ridiculous dreams as men landing on the moon and disposable diapers. Mom has so much knowledge and practical experience in this area that she has been awarded two honorary degrees: M.D.D. (Master of Droopy Drawers) and Ph.Ds (Professor of Home Diaper Services).

Here are some of her hints:

Many doctors have warned that bleach causes diaper rashes, but people still use bleach because they think it is the only way to get diapers white and fresh-smelling. Borax will do the same job without irritating the baby's skin. When the baby is small, fill the diaper pail half full of water and add ½ cup of borax. This whitens the diapers and keeps them sweet-smelling between washings. As the baby begins to crawl, a pail full of water is a pool full of fun, so the diapers have to be soaked in the washing machine overnight or for a few hours before washing. Use hot water and add ½ cup of baking soda to the wash cycle for extra whitening power.

Fabric softeners should be used for diapers only occasionally. It makes the diapers less absorbent, and some babies are allergic to the perfumes. In the final rinse, add one cup of white vinegar. This will break down any remaining soapy residue.

Do not iron diapers. Not only is this a ridiculous waste of time, but it also makes them less absorbent.

30

Cornstarch is still one of the best bottom-healers and it will also help prevent diaper rash. In fact, many of the leading baby product manufacturers are now advertising that their powders contain cornstarch. Mom used to keep a large salt shaker filled with cornstarch in the laundry room. While she was folding a diaper, she sprinkled the center with the cornstarch. The diapers were always ready to pin on without further fuss.

Baby: unreasonable facsimile
—Jack Herbert

DIAPER PAIL

Buy a large diaper pail that has a tightly fitting lid. Each time the diapers are washed, rinse out the pail. The borax used to soak the diapers in is an effective cleaner. Add ½ cup to a gallon of water and let it soak for ½ hour. Scrub with a terry-cloth rag or scrub brush, rinse, and wipe it dry. The sun makes a good deodorizer and disinfectant, so if you have time, let the diaper pail take a sunbath for a few hours. A sheet of fabric softener such as Bounce in the bottom of the diaper pail will keep it sweet-smelling until wash time.

Sign over the desk of a leading dairy executive: **All that I am I owe to udders.**

MILK

Babies love to squirt their bottles or even unscrew the caps and dump the milk on any inconvenient spot. If this type of accident happens on a carpet, it will sour and the smell will be overpowering. Saturate the area with

31

club soda. If you have a water-type suction vacuum, remove the club soda with that. If you don't own that type of vacuum, use terry-cloth rags. Rinse the carpet with a vinegar-and-water solution and wipe it dry.

For mild stains on clothes, soak them in cold water. Pretreat with a prewash stain remover, then rinse. If the stain persists, sponge it with a cleaning solvent.

STUFFED ANIMALS

These cute little toys cannot be washed. In a large grocery bag add 2 to 3 cups of yellow cornmeal. Drop in the stuffed toy and shake. Remove it from the bag and shake or brush the toy to remove any remaining cornmeal.

WATERPROOF PANTS

Machine-wash with the diapers. Do not put them in the dryer. Air-dry outside if possible.

3 Creative Accidents

The only time a child is as good as gold is on April 15.
—Ivern Boyett

Oh, the creative accidents of children—there is nothing so horrible and yet so hilarious! Once I was complaining to my sister about my four-year-old son. He had been playing Tarzan on my swag drapes. I found him on the floor of the front room, screaming and kicking. He was pinned down by the drapery rod and buried underneath mountains of cloth. It was difficult for my sister to sympathize through her tears of laughter.

Weeks later she didn't think it was so funny when *her* four-year-old son took his brand-new birthday gift, a hammer, and hammered some nails in two boards and then quietly placed them behind his dad's brand-new car tires. Daddy didn't see them, but he felt them as he backed out of the driveway. I offered my condolences between bursts of giggles.

When I come across a creative accident I keep things in perspective by asking myself this question: "Is this an irritation or a tragedy?" Tragedies I define as death, disease, divorce, and disasters. If what has happened doesn't fall under one of these headings, I classify it as an irritation and I have learned that every irritation has a lot of humor in it if you just give it a little time. (Of course, it is always funnier if it happens to someone else or if there is a quick remedy for the problem.)

In this chapter are some solutions to common cleanable creative accidents that parents of active, intelligent children often have to face. Use caution when attempting stain removal. Always test cleaners on a small, hidden area first. This is especially important on delicate fabrics and wallpapers.

When a child asks difficult questions, invention is the necessity of Mother.

CRAYONS

I think scribbling on the walls must be the oldest undiagnosed house-cleaning problem in the world. Archaeologists have spent thousands of hours examining cave wall artistry with expensive scientific equipment. I have always thought that this was a ridiculous waste of time, energy, and money when any mother could tell them how those scrawls and scribbles got on the wall. It probably happened when mother was busy cooking a dinosaur and the cave kids got into daddy's tools and paints.

Obviously, those poor mothers didn't know of any way to scrub it off, but today there is a cure for almost everything. Try white toothpaste. It contains a detergent and a mildly abrasive substance, such as a finely powdered chalk. Just squeeze the toothpaste on the crayon mark and then scrub it with a damp rag. The only drawback with this solution is that many mothers like to punish their children for scribbling on the walls by making them help scrub it off. For some reason, squirting toothpaste on the wall is almost as much fun as drawing on it.

Silver cream will also remove crayon without hurting the wall. Just put a little dab on a rag and scrub. Canden Company has put out a crayon eraser called Crayerase which can be found next to the crayons in many stores. This is a dry chemical cleaning bar that is very effective in removing crayon on walls and wallpaper. Follow the directions on the label. Use turpentine or lighter fluid as a last resort, because they will remove some of the shine from a glossy wall. Pour a small amount on a terry-cloth rag and scrub.

Some crayons on the market contain a permanent dye. The only way to know if you were unlucky enough to buy this kind is if none of the above remedies work. I once had a masterpiece on my wall that I tried everything on. My wall became dull-looking, but there was still a faint shadow of color

34

that wouldn't go away. Finally we had to repaint. Since then I've gotten smarter and I buy only crayons that are clearly marked *scrubbable*.

Heredity is what you believe in when your child gets A's in school.

CRAYONS IN THE LAUNDRY

I have received many a cry of help from a young mother who opened the dryer to find crayons that had been hiding in one of the children's pockets. One mother called in desperation when a red and green crayon got in with all of her best white clothes, including the cute little blouses she had bought for her daughter's birthday just a few weeks before. Everything was splotched in the bright Christmas colors.

I gave her the recipe we use to remove stains from baby clothes that is found on page 28.

This young mother was so thrilled with the results that she called long distance to thank me. Oh, I love happy endings.

The toughest thing about raising kids is convincing them that you have seniority.

FINGERNAIL POLISH

The only way I know to remove fingernail polish is with acetone, which is the solvent found in fingernail polish remover. Not only will it dissolve fingernail polish but it will also dissolve rayon and some plastics and take paint right off the wall.

35

GLUE

There are many different kinds of glue, and some can never be removed. Check the back of the package for the manufacturer's instructions for cleaning. Fresh glue can be scraped off with a dull knife or washed off with a damp soapy cloth. If the glue is hard, carefully apply drops of hot white vinegar, cleaning solvent such as Thoro or Energine, or fingernail polish remover over the glue. Put an absorbent cloth over this and then pour more of the removal agent over the cloth. Place a bowl upside down over the stain to prevent evaporation. Repeat the process every ten minutes until the glue is soft, then scrape it off, using the edge of a spoon or butter knife. Wash the area with hot water.

FOR A MOUTHY CHILD

God and devil still are wrangling
Which should have him, which repel!
God wants no discord in his heaven
Satan has enough in hell!

GUM

To remove chewing gum from the floor (no-wax, wood, etc.), rub the stained area with ice and then scrape it off with a dull knife.

To get gum out of clothes and carpet, follow the same method, but after scraping off as much as possible, dampen a white rag with a cleaning solvent such as Thoro or Energine and remove any remaining gum.

To remove gum from hair, use cooking oil or peanut butter. Put a small amount in the palm of your hand and work it into the gum and hair, then pick out or comb out any that is left.

INK

Many types of ink stains on clothes can be removed with cheap hair spray. I have read that it works because of the lacquer content and also that it is the rubbing alcohol in the hair spray that does the trick. Since I am not a chemist I don't really care, as long as it works. On clothes, just spray the hair spray on the stain and throw them in the wash.

Ditto fluid will remove ink stains on walls and woodwork. You can buy Ditto fluid from a copy shop or a well-stocked stationery store. Test on a small, hidden area of your wall before attempting stain removal.

———————

Father's comment: "I just want to live long enough to be as much of a nuisance to my children as they have been to me."
—Walter Davenport

———————

KOOL-AID

I received the following letter:

Dear Jill,

I have gold carpet in my home and the grandkids are always spilling red punch or grape juice. I find that regular table salt or any kind of salt will take it right out. What I do is dampen the punch stain with water, dump some salt on the spot and rub it in. I let it sit a few minutes to allow the salt to absorb the punch, then brush it out or vacuum it up. If it doesn't do it the first time I repeat the process. The salt absorbs the color. It works for me every time.

J.J.
Sandy City, Utah

Before my mother or I pass a helpful hint along we try it first, so I called my husband at work and asked him to bring home a package of red Kool-Aid.

"That's all you want?" he asked.

"That's it," I answered.

"What are you going to do with it?"

"I'm going to mix it up," I told him, "and then dump it on the carpet."

This is the same man who has put up with Tang in the dishwasher, Lysol Toilet Bowl Cleaner on the windows, Coke in the toilet, and toothpaste on the wall. It didn't even surprise him. He did, however, request that I use a carpet sample.

I followed directions in the letter and they worked perfectly for fresh Kool-Aid. It was so exciting to see all that red dye soaked up in the salt. I decided to let the Kool-Aid stain stand for several days and then try it. The salt absorbed some of the dye, but the stain was still there. I repeated the process several times, but I still had a red stain on the carpet sample when I gave up.

While I was experimenting I did discover something else that may help others. I accidently spilled the Kool-Aid on the counter top. "If it works on carpet, then why not?" I asked myself. I sprinkled the salt over the stain. The salt absorbed it immediately and the stain was gone.

On clothes, rinse the Kool-Aid out with cold water and then pretreat with a prewash stain remover and wash.

Hint: To remove Kool-Aid mustaches on children's faces, use a little toothpaste on a wet washcloth.

Parents spend half their time worrying about how a child will turn out and the rest of the time wondering when a child will turn in.
—Ted Cook

LIPSTICK

On mirrors and walls use hot water and an SOS pad. A dry-cleaning solvent such as Thoro or Energine will sometimes remove lipstick on walls. Walls require some elbow grease and time. Don't give up too easily.

On tablecloths or clothes, put the lipstick stain between two brown paper bags and iron with a hot iron. On carpets, lay a brown paper bag over the stained area and iron. Change the bags as often as needed. Treat the remaining stain with Fels-Naptha soap or Lava hand soap. Wet the stained area and the soap, then rub the soap into the stain. On carpets, rinse out the soap with a solution of ½ cup of white vinegar to ½ gallon of warm water.

MAGIC MARKERS

There are two types of magic markers, permanent and nonpermanent. If you have young children, my advice is to never permit a permanent magic marker in the house. The nonpermanent types can be removed with cheap hair spray or a prewash stain remover such as Spray 'n Wash. As one mother wrote us, "I bought my children a package of 12 magic markers (water-based) and my young son decided to go on a writing spree all over our front room. I was sick when I saw it. I tried putting a little cleanser on a washcloth and rubbing, but it smeared all over. I used Spray 'n Wash and it removed every trace of magic marker on the couch, chairs and carpet."

After using Spray 'n Wash or hair spray on upholstery or carpets, rinse it out with a solution of ¼ cup of vinegar to ½ gallon of warm water.

Permanent magic markers obviously are much more difficult to remove. After all, they are made to last forever. Ditto fluid, mentioned a few pages back, will sometimes remove permanent magic marker. We have also had some success on clothes with Cutter Insect Repellent Lotion (not the spray). Just rub it in, wait for a few minutes, and rinse it out. Do not use it on any type of vinyl or plastic because it will damage or destroy these materials.

Permanent magic marker on sturdy wall coverings can sometimes be removed by using an SOS pad dipped in Spic and Span and hot water. If you still need more of a power boost, sprinkle cleanser on the SOS pad. Obviously this is going to dull a glossy wall or ruin a delicate wallpaper.

Rainy days are when Mommy's little jewels are only semiprecious.
—*Floyd R. Miller*

PENCIL

On walls, remove pencil marks with a soft eraser or—if the creative artwork covers a large area—use an SOS pad with a solution of hot water and Spic and Span. This may dull the finish. On clothes, pretreat with a prewash stain remover, and wash. If the stain persists, apply a few drops of ammonia to it and pretreat again.

TOILET PAPER HINT

Squash the roll of toilet paper before you put it on the holder. It doesn't unroll quite so easily for young ones, who love to use it for streamers or who want to see just how much toilet paper the toilet will hold before it over-flows.

This I know
Concerning racket:
Homes with children
Seldom lack it.
—*Richard Wheeler*

POISONING:
AN ACCIDENT THAT IS
NEVER HUMOROUS

At the beginning of this chapter I explained how to tell the difference between an irritation and a tragedy. Poisoning is definitely a tragedy, not only because it kills and maims so many of our children each year, but because it is avoidable.

All cleaners should be added to your list of potential poisons. Especially watch out for dishwashing detergents, laundry detergents, prewash stain removers, drain cleaners, cleanser, toilet bowl cleaners, hard-water cleaners, oil furniture polishes, cleaning solvents, rust removers, oven cleaners, and household bleaches.

Keep all these potential poisons in a high, locked cupboard.

———————

Every adult needs a child to teach; it's the way adults learn.
—Frank A. Clark

———————

4 Grandparents & Grandchildren (Golden Age Rules)

Grandchildren are God's way of compensating us for growing old.
—Mary H. Waldrip

I would like to introduce you to a friend of mine, Mrs. Florence Woodbury, or Grandma Woodbury to scores of grandchildren and great-grandchildren and many others who adopted her into their families as a grandma. She is well into her nineties, but if you are so bold as to ask her exact age she just laughs, "I am the same age as my tongue and a little older than my teeth."

I was visiting Grandma Woodbury at her home one day. I said to her, "Mrs. Woodbury, how are you feeling today?" She is sometimes hard of hearing so I wasn't much surprised when she said, "What?"

I leaned a little closer and raised my voice. "How are you feeling today?"

Somehow I missed that mischievous twinkle in her eye, when she looked directly at me and shook her head. "I can't hear you."

Finally in total frustration I shouted, "How are you feeling today?"

"With my hands," she replied through a burst of giggles. "How are *you* feeling today?"

HOCUS FOCUS

My face in the mirror
isn't wrinkled or drawn.

My house isn't dusty.
The cobwebs are gone.
My garden is lovely
And so is my lawn.
I don't think I should
Put my glasses back on!
—Mr. W. K. Smith

Grandma Woodbury told me the cleanest cleaning joke I have heard. It is apparently an antique joke. My eighty-year-old grandmother remembers her father telling a variation of this joke when she was a young girl.

It seems that a man went to the doctor for an examination. When he took off his clothes the doctor exclaimed, "Good heavens, man, don't you ever take a bath?"

The man said in a slow drawl, "Yes sir! Every day I pull out the old tub, fill it full of water and I wash up as far as possible, then I get down the old bucket, fill it full of water, and I wash down as far as possible."

The doctor looked at him again and then quickly ordered, "Well, go home immediately and wash possible!"

The most impressive example of tolerance is a golden wedding anniversary.

Grandmothers are special people in my life and the life of my children. I have had many requests from grandmothers, (including my own mother and grandmother) to write a chapter in this book on coping with little visitors called grandchildren.

Have you ever wondered why grandparents often say, "I love being a grandparent—you can spoil the kids rotten and then send them home"? Well, it's pure and simple revenge against parents who bring their children

43

over to Grandma's and Grandpa's, let them destroy the house, and then drag the kids home with a fond farewell, leaving the disaster behind.

It was just such a situation that inspired this verse:

> I've seen the lights of London.
> I've seen the lights of Rome.
> But the best lights of all
> Are the tail lights of the car
> Taking the grandchildren home.

Here are a few simple rules that may help to ease the tension between the three generations.

Rule 1 (parents): Teach the children the golden age rule: Do not do unto Grandma's and Grandpa's house what you wouldn't do unto our house. This means you must discipline the kids when they swing on the drapes, jump on the couch, and throw the pillows at the crystal glass collection, so that Grandma and Grandpa don't have to look like mean old gorgons when they tell the kids "No." Let Grandma and Grandpa be the good guys in their own home.

One nice thing about growing older is that you and your children eventually wind up on the same side of the generation gap.

Rule 2 (grandparents): Do not expect active, healthy children to sit with their arms folded for two hours when they come to visit. Get some toys for them to play with. If you gave away all of your children's toys, spend a Saturday visiting the garage sales. My mother has a toy cupboard filled with building blocks, Barbie dolls, cars, crayons, and scrap paper. Her outdoor equipment includes two swing sets, a volleyball game, an outdoor Ping-

Pong table, and two teeterbobs. Of course, she also has forty-five grand-children, but we never hear them whine, "I'm bored."

A child is someone who passes through your life and disappears into adulthood.

Rule 3 (parents): Before you leave Grandma's and Grandpa's house, make it a habit to have the children pick up the messes they make. This is good training for the children. You don't want them to think they can go visiting, make a mess, and leave it. The parents of your children's friends may chalk it up to poor parental instruction if the kids don't know how to pick up after themselves. In fact, I have seen mothers ban some of the neighborhood children from their houses because the children have never been taught to pick up after playtime was over. Grandpa's and Grandma's house is the perfect place for training your children properly. After all, it was a good enough place for your own instruction.

Why is it that a person your own age always looks older than you do?

Rule 4 (grandparents): As hard as this may be for you, don't thoroughly clean house before your grandchildren come—wait until after they leave. Your efforts will last many times longer and you won't be nearly so frustrated. Remember that a cookie tastes just as good to your grandchildren whether it is eaten over a dirty carpet or a clean carpet. (*Hint:* My mother has a cookie jar at child level that her grandchildren are welcome to get into anytime they want. One time when we went to visit, the cookie jar was empty. Each one of the children in turn picked up the lid and then quietly put it down exclaiming in disappointment, "No cookies!" It wasn't until

45

then that we realized how important the cookie jar was to the tradition of "going to Grandma's house." Mom vowed never to let the cookie jar be empty again.

Rule 5 (parents and grandparents): Invite each other over often. My dear friend Grandma Woodbury passed away not very long ago. As I sat in the chapel at her funeral I watched the wonderful legacy that was hers—her family. They talked about her rich sense of humor and retold some of her favorite jokes and experiences. They spoke of the treasures in the family antique collection. The collection wasn't worth a lot of money, but every piece in it had a story that Grandma Woodbury eagerly shared with whoever came to visit. This sweet grandma had created pleasant memories and warm feelings in her family. This sharing between the generations is truly important. If the house becomes a little mussed up in the process, just remember that it will always be there to clean, long after the wonderful people in it are gone.

———————

Yesterday is a cancelled check; tomorrow is a promissory note;
today is ready cash—use it.
—Kay Lyons

———————

5 The Undercover Cleaners

Today's society will ignore any type of public misbehavior except getting into the express line with more than ten items.

Many of the best cleaners on the national market go unheralded even though their manufacturers have million-dollar marketing budgets. Why? Well, imagine if you will, the following TV advertisement.

A little girl spots Grandma's Efferdent denture tablets sitting on the cabinet in the bathroom. "Hey, Grandma," she shouts, "I know what these are for."

Grandma rushes in just as the little girl rips open the blue packages and drops two tablets into the toilet. Close-up picture of bubbling and fizzling. "See that cleaning action?" the girl chirps proudly. She brushes the bowl and then quickly flushes.

Grandma's puzzlement turns into a dazzling grin as she announces, "Efferdent makes my toilet as white as my teeth."

Obviously, the Efferdent company would never want its retail customers to associate their tooth tablets (very sanitary) with toilets (oh, my!). Yet Efferdent is one of the best toilet-bowl cleaners around. It is cheap (you can buy half a year's supply for under $4) and safe enough for the youngest aspiring housekeeper in the family to use. The only problem is that it won't take out that crusty hard-water build-up problem. For this you need a pumice stone. I am talking about the one shelved by the foot-care products. It is good for calluses, but it is great for removing mineral build-up in the toilet, sinks, or bathtub.

Here are some more undercover cleaners that just may surprise you.

47

BAKING SODA

If you run out of cleaners, baking soda is also a mild abrasive that will clean tubs and sinks. Dip a damp rag in baking soda and scrub.

To get rid of hard-water stains on a fixture, sprinkle baking soda over it, then pour on some white vinegar. Wrap a terry-cloth rag around the fixture and let it soak for at least an hour. Scrub with a stainless steel pad.

BEER

Gilded mirror frames can be wiped clean with beer. Pour it on a soft rag, rub gently, and wipe dry.

Recession is when your neighbor loses his job.
Depression is when you lose your job.
Panic is when your wife loses her job.

CLUB SODA

This is great for cleaning dull Formica counter tops. Pour undiluted club soda directly on the counter, wash, rinse with warm water, and wipe dry.

To remove stains in the carpet, pour club soda on the stain and scrub. Rinse with a vinegar-and-water solution and wipe as dry as possible.

To put the shine back on a stainless steel sink, rub it with a rag soaked with club soda and wipe the sink dry.

To remove wallpaper glue, which sometimes stains wallpaper after a hanging job, pour club soda on a rag, gently rub the glue away, then wipe it dry.

COKE

48

This contains phosphoric acid; read the ingredients label. To remove a stain from a toilet bowl (that hasn't been permanently damaged by using harsh toilet-bowl cleaners), pour a bucket of water down the bowl or use a toilet-bowl plunger (plumber's helper). This forces the water level below the ring and makes it accessible to work on. If the ring isn't too bad, pour a can of Coke around the stain. Let it soak for a few minutes, then brush.

To remove old grease from a driveway, first soak it up with kitty litter, sand, or sawdust. Sweep and then pour enough Coke over the stain to cover it. Let it soak for at least twenty minutes, but do not let it dry. Then brush it out with a patio broom or scrub brush.

Pour Coke over the car battery to remove battery acid.

CUTTER INSECT REPELLENT LOTION (NOT THE SPRAY)

This will sometimes remove permanent magic marker from clothes. Rub it in the stain. Wait a few minutes, then rinse. Do not use it on vinyl or plastic.

If you are a self-starter your boss doesn't have to be a crank.
—Buck Herzog

DENTURE TABLETS

Drop two Efferdent or Polydent tablets in the toilet bowl, let them dissolve, brush and flush.

DENTURE CREAM

Put on a toothbrush and scrub the grout in the shower. It really whitens and brightens it.

DISHWASHING DETERGENT (FOR AUTOMATIC DISHWASHERS)

For cruddy shower floors, wet the floor and sprinkle with powdered dishwasher soap. Scrub with a nylon brush or soap-filled pad.

DISHWASHING ANTISPOTTING AGENT (JET DRY)

To clean those impossible-to-reach windows, put 2 to 3 tablespoons of liquid dishwashing soap and 1 tablespoon of Jet Dry in a spray bottle with a hose attachment that is used to spray insecticides. Fill the spray bottle with water, attach it to the hose, and spray one section of the window at a time. Rinse that section immediately with clean water. The water will sheet off, so there is no need to dry the window.

Some people are born busybodies. They have an interferiority complex.

EPSOM SALTS

Add 1 cup of this to the final rinse when washing sheers to replace body often lost in the washing process.

GELATIN

To keep wrinkles out of Dacron sheers and give them body, dissolve 1 package of unflavored gelatin in 1 cup of boiling water and then add it to the final rinse after washing.

GOOP (HAND CLEANER)

To remove the greasy finger marks on kitchen cupboard, put Goop on a terry-cloth rag and scrub.

HAIR SPRAY

Cheap hair spray will remove ball point pen stains from fabric. Spray the stain and launder.

KETCHUP

Polishes copper. Pour it on and scrub with an SOS pad.

KITTY LITTER

The fresh grease spills on concrete driveways can be cleaned with kitty litter. Sprinkle enough on the concrete to cover the stain. Rub it in with the ball of your shoe or a patio broom and then sweep it up.

LAVA (HAND SOAP)

To remove greasy smudges around the cupboard handles, dip a wet rag in Murphy's Oil Soap or Lin-Sol, then rub Lava soap on it and scrub. If the stain is really tough, follow the same procedure, but rub the Lava on a wet Scotch-Brite pad.

If life hands you a lemon, make lemonade.

LEMON EXTRACT

To get rid of a foul smell in the refrigerator, add a teaspoon of lemon extract to the wash water.

LEMONS

Squeeze a fresh lemon over a stain on a Formica counter top. Let it soak for half an hour, then sprinkle some baking soda over the lemon juice. Scrub with a terry-cloth rag, rinse, and wipe dry.

Light rust can be removed with a fresh lemon cut in half and dipped in salt. Rub it in and rinse it out.

Fix the mistake, not the blame!

LEMON OIL FURNITURE POLISH (LIQUID—NOT SPRAY)

To put a shine back on a shiny Formica counter top, use lemon oil furniture polish once a week. Put the lemon oil on a rag and rub it on the counter, then use another rag and wipe it dry.

For grease spots on the oven window, put the oven door down and coat it with a thin layer of lemon oil. Let this set for an hour to loosen the grease. Scrub with an SOS pad or stainless steel pad. Make sure all the oil is washed off or the oven will smoke the next time it is used.

For grease spots behind the stove on shiny Formica, put a layer of lemon oil on the area and scrub with a stainless steel pad or SOS pad. Rinse and wipe dry.

To remove mild hard-water build-up on Formica, tile, and ceramic showers, pour a generous amount of lemon oil on a soft rag and wipe the shower walls. It will take several applications to cover the whole shower. With a clean cloth, rub the shower dry. *Do not put lemon oil on the floor of the shower or bathtub because the oil will make it slippery.*

LIME

To remove onion or garlic smells from your cutting board, slice a lime and rub it into the board.

MEAT TENDERIZER

To remove blood stains from washable fabrics, wet the stain and sprinkle on meat tenderizer. Rub the stained fabric together and launder.

The saying "There is no use crying over spilled milk" was written before milk was $2.00 a gallon.

MILK

Add 1 cup of milk to the final rinse when washing sheers. This will put the crispness back into them.

MENTHOLATUM AND MAYONNAISE

To remove water rings on real wood furniture, rub them with mentholatum or mayonnaise, let set for eight hours, then lightly sand with a dry Scotch-Brite pad and polish with oil.

RUBBING ALCOHOL

To shine bathtub and sink fixtures, put rubbing alcohol on a rag, scrub, and wipe dry.

To remove spots in a stainless steel sink, scrub it with a terry-cloth rag dipped in rubbing alcohol.

A great window cleaner can be made from 2 tablespoons of rubbing alcohol in 2 quarts of water.

To clean a chandelier the easy way, put 2 teaspoons of rubbing alcohol and 1 pint warm water in a spray bottle and drench the chandelier. Let it drip dry. (Be sure the lights are off and cool.)

Stains in nonwashable upholstery can sometimes be eliminated by sponging with undiluted rubbing alcohol. Try this in an inconspicuous place first.

SALT

To recondition sponges, soak them in 2 tablespoons of salt to 2 quarts of water, then wash them in the washing machine with the towels.

Shower floors can be cleaned by mixing 2 tablespoons of salt and ½ cup of turpentine. Make a paste out of it, rub it on the floor, scrub with a nylon brush, rinse, and wipe dry.

Fresh Kool-Aid stains can be removed from the carpet by sprinkling salt over the stain. It will absorb the stain. Vacuum the carpet and rinse with a vinegar-and-water solution.

Absorb grease spots in fabric or carpet with salt.

Marriage is like the army. Everyone complains, but you'd be surprised at how many reenlist.
—Record, *Columbia, S.C.*

STARCH

To give a tile floor a shiny, glazed look, add ½ cup of powdered clothes starch to 1 gallon of warm water. Apply a very thin layer in the same way you would apply wax, and let it dry.

TANG (INSTANT BREAKFAST DRINK)

Great for hard-water stains or hard-water build-up in dishwashers. Wet the stain and sprinkle Tang over it. Let it stand for one hour, then load the dishes, add the dishwasher detergent, and run it through a normal cycle. If you have trouble with spotting on dishes or glasses, add ½ teaspoon Tang to the dishwasher detergent every time you wash the dishes.

TOOTHPASTE

54   To remove a water ring on furniture, coat the ring with white toothpaste

and let it set for eight hours. Lightly sand with a dry Scotch-Brite pad and polish with oil.

To remove crayon from a washable surface, put white toothpaste on a terry-cloth rag and scrub.

VANILLA

To get rid of a foul smell in the refrigerator, add a teaspoon of vanilla to the wash water.

Meat prices keep many a family in a perpetual stew.

VINEGAR

Put ½ cup of vinegar in an ice-cube tray, fill the tray with water, and freeze. Grind the vinegar cubes down the Disposall once a week. The ice cubes sharpen the blades and the vinegar cleans and freshens the Disposall.

To clean or remove stains from a colored porcelain sink or a stainless steel sink, pour white vinegar over the stain and scrub with a Scotch-Brite pad.

To restore the bright clear color of aluminum pans that have discolored, pour in enough vinegar to cover the stained area, bring it to a boil, turn down the heat and let it simmer for five minutes. Let the vinegar soak in the pan for an hour after the burner is turned off and then wash the pan.

To remove burned-on crud in pots and pans, cover the burn with water and then add ¼ cup of vinegar. Bring this to a boil and turn off the heat. Add 1 teaspoon of baking soda and let it stand until cool. If the burned crud is really bad, scrape off as much as possible and repeat.

Add ⅛ cup white vinegar to the rinse water in your washing machine. This breaks down the soap residue so that the clothes, especially the dark clothes, look brighter. There is a slight vinegar smell while the clothes are still wet, but it goes away as soon as they dry.

Vinegar will remove fish and onion odors from dishes, utensils, and hands.

A line left from letting down a hem sometimes can be removed by sponging it with vinegar and then pressing it with an iron on the wrong side of the fabric.

Clean your no-wax floor with a solution of 1 tablespoon of white vinegar to 1 gallon of water, instead of using harsh commercial cleaners that will remove the no-wax shine. Vinegar is an excellent cleaner for normal dirt build-up on a no-wax floor and it is cheap to use.

Discoloration of clothes caused by perspiration stains and soft-drink and wine stains can sometimes be remedied by sponging them with white vinegar.

Hot vinegar used with an SOS pad will remove hard-water stains on glasses or bottles. Some people even use the vinegar from their dill pickles to shine the fruit bottle. It saves money.

To clean up animal stains on carpets, pour white vinegar on the spot and continually blot up the moisture. Lay a dry towel over the stain, put a heavy object on it, and leave it overnight.

To clean discolored or stained aluminum, or stainless steel pans, make a paste out of red wine, vinegar, and salt, and scrub with an SOS or Scotch-Brite pad.

Money won't buy happiness, but it will pay the salaries of a large research staff to study the problem.
—Bill Vaughan

WORCESTERSHIRE SAUCE

This polishes brass. Put it directly on the brass object, scrub it with an SOS pad, rinse, and wipe dry.

WALNUTS

To hide light surface scratches on wood furniture, take the meat out of a walnut and rub it into the scratch. Scratches can also be filled with a matching color of eyebrow pencil or a permanent magic marker.

————————

A minister, attempting eulogy in a funeral sermon: "We have here only the shell; the nut is gone."

————————

YOGURT (unflavored)

This is the best cleaner for piano keys. Rub it on and wipe it dry.

6 Holiday Cleanup

THANKSGIVING

JUST LIKE THE PILGRIMS

Thanksgiving is a day that we celebrate
By eating just like the pilgrims ate.
There's a self-basting turkey roasted to prime
With a magic red button that pops when it's time,

Stove-top stuffing with premeasured spices,
Cranberries served whole or in slices,
Potatoes whipped with electric beaters,
Presweetened Kool-Aid poured by the liters,

Fresh frozen vegetables cooked to perfection,
In a microwave with built-in convection,
Pillsbury rolls baked on a Teflon pan,
Pumpkin pies straight from the can.

And when we're all stuffed and the feast is gone,
The dishwasher is stacked and the TV turned on.
Yes, traditions are great, so I'm really glad
We have a Thanksgiving just like the pilgrims had.
—Jill C. Major and Donna J. Chapla

The problem with Thanksgiving is that the turkeys at the table gobble up the food and leave the head housekeeper (who is usually the person who started cooking the feast at 6:00 A.M.) with dirty dishes, greasy pots and pans, and a picked-over carcass. I suggest that this year you ruffle their feathers! No matter how much they squawk, give each member of your family a chore to do. For example, let the children clear and wash the silverware, the teenagers scrape and wash the plates, and the men scrub the pots and pans. "What will the women be doing?" you ask. I think it is about their turn to supervise, and watch the football game.

If the family needs a little extra incentive, steal the plug from the TV or lock up the pumpkin pies until the work is done. The only way to spell relief from the post-Thanksgiving disaster is c-o-o-p-e-r-a-t-i-o-n!

CHRISTMAS

SEND YOUR ELVES . . . PLEASE!

Jolly Old St. Nicholas—
Christmas cleaning is a chore
With smashed ornaments, crushed candy canes,
And pine needles on my floor.

When the clock is striking twelve
And everyone's gone to bed,
I'm still scrubbing bowls and pans
From making candy and nut bread.

All the stockings you will find
Hanging neatly in a row.
It's the only tidy place in my house,
Because I've done nothing but sew.

Johnny will get his pair of skates,
But I really must confess
That Suzy will never get that doll
That eats real food and makes a mess!

Jolly Old St. Nicholas,
Lean your ear this way.
If you really want to make Christmas great,
Send your elves to help me for a day!
—Jill C. Major

Did you know that it is entirely possible to have a beautiful home during the Christmas holidays even when, because of all the extra hustle and bustle, your house is a cleaning calamity?

I decided last year to follow the experts' admonitions to "start early." I reasoned that if I could get all my housecleaning done at the beginning of the season, I would have plenty of time for shopping and partying.

One morning I sprang from my bed and immediately got to work sorting out the laundry into neat little bundles; then, after plopping the first batch into the washer, I started on the kitchen. Things were beginning to take shape when the sound of mischievous giggles reached my ears. I ran down the stairs, but it was too late. My two boys had gathered up all those little untidy bundles of laundry and placed them in one large, neat pile. Apparently the pile was rather puny by their standards, so they decided to add all the clean clothes they could find, just for good measure. When I opened the door, one little elf was standing on the hamper, ready for takeoff. The other little elf had just made a soft landing.

While I was sorting the laundry again, my sons decided to be helpful and shovel out the fireplace so that Santa Claus could make a clean entrance. Once they got the ashes out on the hearthstone they created a miniature highway system by driving their cars and trucks through the ashes, across the carpet and up the couches and chairs.

As the poem goes, they were "all tarnished with ashes and soot," so I stripped them down and put them in the bathtub, thinking they couldn't get into much trouble in that confined space. When I checked on them a few minutes later, they were up to their chins in bubbles.

"How did you do that?" I screeched. Byron was glad to demonstrate how a bottle of shampoo combined with rapid agitation of the feet made the bubbles grow higher and higher.

All day long I was just one step behind the next mess. Soon my older children started trailing home from school. It was time to start dinner and even though I had worked all day, the house was in worse shape than it had been that morning. If the Promised Valley Playhouse had held tryouts for the role of Scrooge that afternoon, I could have won it without even an audition. Bah! Humbug! I was grouchy.

"Mom, could you help me with this?" Christopher asked as he handed me his cub scout book. The page was open to the section on conservation. I quickly glanced at the paragraph he was pointing to. The instructions read: "Think of six ways to make where you live beautiful. Talk with your den leader or parents about which one you will do and then do it."

"The best way I can think of to make this place more beautiful is for you to get in there and clean up your room," I snapped.

"Never mind," he quickly decided. "I can do it myself."

Fifteen minutes later he returned and proudly handed his book to me. There scrawled were these six suggestions for home beautification: 1. Be nice. 2. Be good. 3. Be happy. 4. Have fun. 5. Be kind. 6. Love everybody.

I still think that getting the house cleaned early is an excellent idea (if you have a young family, take a lesson from my story and tackle those things that the kids can't undo for at least two weeks, such as cleaning the oven or the refrigerator, or de-cobwebbing the chandelier) but no matter what your house looks like, make sure that the number-one spot on your priority list is always to keep your home a beautiful place to live in during the Christmas holiday and all year round.

The best gift of all is the presence of a happy family
all wrapped up in each other.

EASTER

Many traditions have unknown origins, unknown meanings, and they make very little sense, but because they are traditions we carry them on. Let me illustrate with a story how this happens.

Once there was a young mother who was preparing a roast for her family's dinner. She carefully cut the roast in half and put it in her big roaster pan. Her sweet little son was watching.

"Mommy, why do you have to cut the meat in half?" he asked.

"Because my mother always cut it in half," explained Mother.

"But why did Grandma cut it in half?" asked the boy.

This made Mother stop and think, so she called Grandma on the phone and asked the same question. Grandma answered, "I don't know. I guess because my mother always used to do it that way."

By now Grandma was curious too, so she called up Great-Grandma and asked, "Why did you always cut the roast in half before you cooked it?"

Great-Grandma answered, "Because I only had a small pan when you were growing up and I had to cut the meat in half to make it fit."

And that is how traditions get passed down. The reason I am explaining all of this is that I would like to permanently ban an Easter tradition: Easter-basket grass! I don't know when it got started that the Easter eggs had to be nestled in a soft bed of shredded green artificial grass, but it is the worst holiday cleaning catastrophe since needle-dropping Christmas trees. Easter grass is strewn from one end of the house to the other and when you try to clean it up, it wraps around the vacuum brush and has to be removed strand by strand.

I suggest that you use crumpled green napkins, or green tissue paper, to line the basket—or start a new tradition and have the nest lined with artificial snow—*cotton.* In many areas spring has been so much like winter that the snow wouldn't even seem out of place.

Easter-egg dyeing is another messy tradition, but I love it. Remember to put lots of newspaper under the work area. Have the children put on their old paint clothes. The dye is generally nonstaining, but who wants to take a chance? If there is a spill on the carpet, absorb it quickly with salt.

If you were put on trial for being a Christian, would there be enough evidence to convict you?

HALLOWEEN

Halloween is supposed to be the scariest day of the year, but the second most terrifying day of the year is the day after Halloween. That's when you have to clean up after all the little spooks. Here are some of the most common problems and their solutions:

Windows adorned with bar-soap drawings: Scrub with very hot water and an SOS pad, then wash with any basic window cleaner.

Shaving cream embellishments: Wash with a cleaning solution of 1 gallon of cool water with 1 tablespoon of vinegar added. The water will become very soapy, so change it frequently.

Eggs: On hard surfaces such as windows or brick, soak with hot water, then scrape off the residue with a razor blade or a dull knife. Scrub the surface with a nylon brush and hot soapy water. On clothes, scrape off as much as possible and soak in cold water. Pretreat with a prewash stain-remover and wash in warm water.

Makeup: For easier removal, use cold cream liberally before applying makeup.

Even much worse than a storm or a riot
Is a bunch of kids who are suddenly quiet.
—Floyd R. Miller

While Christmas, Thanksgiving, Easter, and Halloween present their own unique cleaning problems, there are some messes that seem to come with every holiday.

Candy stains: Soak the clothing (or whatever fabric) in warm water with a little detergent added. Pretreat with a prewash stain-remover and rinse.

Chocolate stains: Soak in cold water, then pretreat with a prewash stain-remover.

Candle wax: Solidify the wax by rubbing it with an ice cube, then scrape off as much as possible with a dull knife. If the wax has dripped on the carpet or other flat surface, place a brown paper bag (large grocery bag) over the wax and hold a hot iron on it for a few seconds to absorb the wax. Repeat, using a clean bag each time until the stain is gone. If the wax is on clothes, tablecloths, and so on, follow the same directions except to sandwich the cloth between *two* pieces of brown paper to protect the ironing board cover. (Caution: Do not use an iron on plastic or vinyl.)

Transparent tape used to secure decorations: On windows, soften the glue by applying a hot wet rag to the tape. (Use a lukewarm rag on a cold window, since a hot rag may break it.) Carefully scrape the tape off with a razor blade. Any remaining glue can be removed with a cleaning solvent such as Thoro. Transparent tape can be removed from the refrigerator by using the same method, but do not use a razor blade. On walls, use a warm iron and press the tape or heat the tape by using a hand-held hair dryer, then peel it off. Any remaining glue will come off with a cleaning solvent.

To hang decorations: Do not use masking tape. It is much more difficult to remove from surfaces.

7 Clutter— the Battle of the Bulge

Eat, drink and be merry, for tomorrow we diet!

People often find themselves depressed because they are constantly losing the battle of the bulge. This isn't a book on weight control, so I don't mean the type of bulge that can be corrected with a new girdle or by calorie-counting.

I am referring to clothes closets that are packed tighter than fans at the World Series; cupboards that are stuffed to overflowing with hamburger presses, hot dog steamers, crepe makers, doughnut bakers, and other small specialized appliances; toy chests that no longer can be closed because of an overabundance of Star Wars and Fisher-Price toys; and hall closets that are as prone to avalanches as the snow-covered mountains.

Right now is the time to help your house shape up by putting it on a clutter-free diet. The main rule to remember in reducing clutter is: If no one has used the item for three years, store it out of the way, or better yet, get rid of it and let it clutter up someone else's house.

Clutter is the things worth saving but not yet put away, deposited on top of the things that are not worth saving but not yet thrown away, which have settled next to the things you just aren't sure what to do with.
—Jill C. Major

KITCHEN

The kitchen cupboards are usually the worst problem, so attack them first. Small specialized appliances go in and out of style as fast as a teenager's wardrobe. Remember the fondue parties? When was the last time you used your fondue maker? Is it stuck way in the back of the cupboard somewhere? Some appliances are used only a couple of times a year, like that yogurt maker you just had to have. Do you still make yogurt for your family or do you cheat and buy the store-bought stuff? Then there is the appliance that we either buy or are given as a gift. We try it out just once, hate it, and never use it again. I know a man who got an electric potato peeler one Christmas. The first time he used it, peelings flew like unguided missiles all over the kitchen. It has been sitting in the same cupboard drawer now for over ten years. Cupboard space is valuable, so save it for items that are used frequently.

Junk: Something you keep ten years and then throw away two weeks before you need it.
—Gloria Ray

If it doesn't work, get it fixed or get rid of it (this doesn't include husbands or children). Some people save those broken appliances for their children, so when they get married or go away to college in the distant future they will have a good start on their new life. Do you really think those kids are going to want that toaster that toasts one side of the bread or the waffle iron that hasn't been used for years because the waffles stick to it every time? By the time some of our children grow up they will be cooking with solar energy (computerized in some way, of course) and our appliances will be as old-fashioned as a coal stove.

After you make room in your cupboards, clear off the counters and put away some of those convenience appliances that make it so inconvenient to find convenient counter space to work on.

If you want to make an easy job mighty hard, just keep putting it off.
—Olin Miller

Go through the kitchen drawers. There are items in them that you never use. A friend had a party in which she set the table using all the little "freebie" gadgets that she had received at Rubbermaid and Tupperware parties throughout the years in place of the silverware. It was hilarious to try to eat soup and salad with these objects, but it was even more fun as we tried to guess what each specialty tool was made for. Even the hostess couldn't remember how to use some of them.

Many homes have a recipe drawer where all the clipped-out and torn-out recipes have been deposited for future reference. The only problem is that recipes that have been tried and loved are mixed up with the never-been-tried recipes and it is impossible to find the favorites. Go through the drawer and separate the recipes. Put those that haven't been tried in a box somewhere else in the house. When you are in the mood to try a different taste treat you will have them handy, but in the meantime they won't be cluttering up the drawer. Copy on recipe cards those your family likes and file them for easy retrieval.

A dieter's fondest wish is to be weighed and found wanting.
—Walter Winchell

Almost every family I know has a junk drawer. This may surprise you, but I think that this is not only necessary but is great. Who wants to take every paper clip, pencil, and screw that manages to run away, back to its proper place? We would never get through with our housework. Every week or two go through the drawer and put away the accumulated items.

MAIL

Do you realize that if you receive only two pieces of mail a day, not including Sundays, each year you would have collected over 600 pieces of mail? Of course, most of us don't receive two pieces of mail a day—rather, we get four or five or more pieces of mail a day. Many times this gets scattered all over the house on the counter tops or the dressers. Make a commitment to take care of your mail just as soon as you remove it from the mailbox. Throw away the garbage mail. Put the bills in a special place you have reserved just for bills. File your bank statements and other important documents for easy retrieval.

One of the hardest problems is what to do with sentimental mail. When the children receive cards or letters from grandparents we make sure they are dated and then save them in a large 8 × 11-inch envelope with the child's name on it. When they leave home they can take this envelope with them and let it clutter up their house.

My mother has a scrapbook for each of her children's families. All the cards, letters, and pictures that her grandchildren send go in that family's scrapbook. The books are left out on a shelf where the grandchildren can easily reach them. There are twenty years of memories in those books, which make up a fun history of each family. They keep the grandchildren entertained for hours when they go to visit Grandma's house.

If at first you don't succeed, you are running about average.
—M. H. Alderson

SCHOOL PAPERS

Another paper problem is the work that the children bring home. One person that Mom works for has four married children. She never threw away a single school paper and they are still stacked in boxes under the bed. That bed takes twenty-five minutes to clean under.

I'm just not that sentimental. I have a drawer in the kitchen that the children put all the papers in. After Ken or I have looked over the papers we save them for a week. At the end of the week I take out any special work, put that in their envelope (described under mail) and throw away the rest.

Income tax forms: Blankity-blanks

CLOSETS

Closets should be used for everyday-wear clothes, not for storage. Honestly, most people have so many clothes in their closets that they could go through three more depressions without buying any more! Some fashion experts say that clothes stay in style for about three years. It is true that the style cycle does repeat itself. My teenage daughter is wearing the same shirt styles this year that my older brothers wore in the 1960s. However, popular colors, fabrics, and brand names change enough that you may not feel comfortable wearing them when the style does return. In the meantime they clog up the closets and waste limited space.

Some people have two or three wardrobes in different sizes, depending on how well they are sticking to their current diet. Children outgrow their clothes so fast that just about the time you think you've caught up with them you look down and can see their pant legs dusting the top of their socks. Remove the clothes that don't fit and store them somewhere else.

If you have younger children to pass the clothes down to, place them in boxes or sacks and label each container according to size and whether it is for a male or female. Then when the children grow into the clothes you can just take down one container instead of searching through the entire storage room. This chore is so tedious and exhausting that often the clothes are outgrown by the second child before they are found. Shoes should not be passed down from child to child. Podiatrists tell us that many of our adult foot pains are caused by shoes that did not fit properly when we were children.

69

Coats not only clutter up the closet, but the whole house as well when children come in from their activities and drape them over a chair or on the floor. For some reason, if coats have to go on hangers in the closet they never get hung up. A coat rack that is at child level near the back door usually solves this problem. I took a two-by-four, cut it four feet long and covered it with leftover wallpaper that matched the covering of the rest of the wall. With the help of a drill and a screwdriver I mounted clothes hooks on it and hung it on the wall behind the back door. We use this not only for coats but also for the children's book bags.

For wet boots a kitty-litter box (brand new, never-been-used type) under the coat rack serves as a good holding tray. The children soon learn to peel off their boots at the back door instead of tromping through the house leaving little mud puddles everywhere. Mother doesn't have to constantly hound them to pick up stray boots lying around, and when the children want to go outside they always know where their boots are.

While you are going through your closets, be sure to take out all the clothes that need mending, are stained, or haven't been worn because they need ironing and you can't remember where you put the ironing board. Take care of the wearable ones and get rid of the rest.

The wishbone will never replace the backbone.
—Will Henry

TOYS

Make sure the kids are not around when you tackle the toys, because they immediately fall in love again with anything you want to give away. Try putting half of their toys in storage. When the kids start complaining "We don't have anything to do," rotate the toys. This method not only brings relief to bulging rooms, but it is just like Christmas again when toys that haven't been played with for a while suddenly reappear.

BOOKS

Having more books than book shelves adds to the clutter problem. Libraries and thrift stores run by churches and other charitable organizations love donations of this type, and it is also a tax write-off for you. I sent all of my husband's old textbooks to the local library. They were thrilled and my husband didn't feel so bad when he knew he still had visitation and check-out rights.

To keep books from stacking up again, try one of the book-trading stores, swap books with a neighbor, and/or use the local library.

MAGAZINES AND NEWSPAPERS

Old newspapers and magazines are also a nuisance. If you haven't had time to read a magazine after it is six months old or a newspaper when it's a week old, give up and get rid of it. Many nonprofit organizations, such as the scouts, collect old newspapers for funds. Some thrift stores also like donations of magazines. If all else fails, clip out your favorite recipes, coupons, and articles, then throw the magazine or newspaper away.

Internal Revenue Service to nervous citizen: "Let's begin with where you claim depreciation on your wife."

GRANDMA'S CLUTTER BOX

In our family my mother keeps a clutter box in which all of her children can deposit their good outgrown clothes and other reusable items. As the families visit, they go through the box and take out whatever their family can use. The older cousins have fun seeing that almost brand-new favorite shirt they had to give up when it got too tight, worn by a younger member of the family.

CLUTTER INTAKE

Once your house has shaped up, continue to watch its clutter intake. Before you buy something ask yourself, "Where am I going to put this and will it add to the beauty of my new slimmer, trimmer home or will it be the beginning of a new creeping bulge?"

Like all diets, this one is hard to begin and even harder to stick with. There isn't an Overclutterers Anonymous or a Clutter Watchers' Organization to help you, so you are on your own. Good luck!

Wise people put aside 10 percent of the money they get and 90 percent of the free advice.

P.S.—Please read the quote above. Although the advice in this chapter isn't free (it cost you the price of the book), if you are comfortable in your cluttered home, ignore 90 percent of this chapter and turn to the next page.

8 The Energy Crisis

He who is always blowing a fuse is usually in the dark.
—Franklin P. Jones

I have decided to nominate my son for a Nobel Prize. He solved a universal mystery that has stumped the greatest scientific minds in the world since the beginning of time; he has figured out the source of a young mother's infinite energy.

Chris has always been a whiz at electricity. He likes to plug in the vacuum and suck up all the pennies in his piggy bank or plug in the toaster and toast two loaves of bread for a snack.

One day he was sitting on the counter stool watching me very intently as I talked on the phone. I had my shoulder cranked up and my neck kinked down so that the phone was pinned in a good talking and listening position and my hands were free to do the dishes, wash the table, clean the cupboards, and sweep the floor. I kept interrupting my conversation to ask him what he needed, but he just stared at me and answered, "Nothing."

The next morning Chris popped into my bedroom bright and early with his usual good morning greeting, "I'm hungry, Mom."

I replied by grunting, moaning, and pulling the covers over my head.

My daughter was right behind him. "What's wrong with Mom?" she asked.

Chris looked at me and then he looked at the phone. It took him only a few seconds to compute the answer. (It is a good thing his mind gears are not fueled by his belly or he would never have made this great discovery before breakfast.) In an authoritative tone he informed his sister, "She hasn't been plugged in yet!"

73

A modern home is one in which a switch regulates everything but the children.

Personal energy is sometimes tough to come by but at least we don't have to pay by the kilowatt-hour for it. The electric company figures out how much money you owe them each month by how many kilowatt-hours you consume. A kilowatt-hour is 1000 watts of electricity delivered to your home for one hour. So that 100-watt light bulb you use as a night light for the kids for 10 hours equals one kilowatt. The national average cost per kilowatt-hour is now about .0675, and since it is difficult to make payment in fractions of a penny I have rounded that to 7 cents.

If you pay the national average per kilowatt-hour, it costs you 7 cents to give your children that added security of the 100-watt light bulb each night, or about $25.55 a year. Your cost per kilowatt-hour may be higher or lower. You can determine what you are paying per kilowatt-hour by dividing the total cost of your last bill (do not include taxes) by the number of kilowatts used.

When parents stop wondering why children don't turn out lights, they're apt to begin wondering why they do.
—Franklin P. Jones

How many of your energy dollars go to cleaning your house? The following figures are based on 7 cents a kilowatt-hour.

The electric clothes dryer costs 27 cents a load if you are drying on a regular cycle, but only 21 cents a load if you are drying on a permanent press cycle. The electric motor for the gas dryer costs only 1½ cents per load, but of course you must pay for the gas in addition to that. Your washer is much more economical to run than the dryer (if you don't include the cost of the water). It costs about 2 pennies a load. The vacuum cleaner is really a bargain. At a little more than 2 cents to use it for 30 minutes, we who have nothing else to do can afford to vacuum all day. Five hours of slaving away ironing our family's clothes costs only 17½ cents, but if we watch five hours of soap operas (or basketball, for our gentlemen housekeepers) on a tube-type color television while we are ironing we must add an additional 12 cents to the electric company's price tag. If you really wanted to save money on ironing day you could watch the same amount of TV on a solid-state color TV for 7 cents, or on a black-and-white solid-state for 2 cents.

If your spouse is a real tightwad and you have been trying to get a dishwasher but the argument has been "It costs too much to run," you may explain that the experts say that one dishwasher load per day usually uses less hot water (only 10 gallons if you do not prerinse with hot water before loading the dishwasher) and therefore costs less than washing three meals of dishes by hand (which uses approximately 5 gallons for each meal's dishes.) The electricity is also cheap at 7 cents a load, using the drying unit. If you are on a really tight budget, turn the drying unit off and it costs just under 4 cents a load.

A conventional electric oven that you have to clean with ammonia or a caustic oven cleaner costs 7 cents an hour to bake your favorite cake, but if you can get your hands on a self-cleaning oven, it costs less than 6 cents an hour because of the extra insulation needed for the self-cleaning unit. However, that self-cleaning feature costs you 17½ cents every time you use it for one hour. (Considering the high cost of oven cleaner, this is truly the bargain of the century and a real energy saver for you!)

The cost of those kilowatt-hours really starts to add if you have a refrigerator or freezer with automatic defrost. A 14 × 16 cubic-foot automatic defrosting refrigerator/freezer with a top freezer unit costs $9.94 a month to run. You can get some superinsulated models that cost $7.70 a month to run. Its counterpart with partial automatic defrost (meaning you have to do part of the work) costs only $5.81 cents a month to run. You can see the same differences between the automatic-defrost freezers and the do-it-yourself manual-defrost freezers. An upright automatic-defrost 15 × 16 cubic-foot freezer costs $11 a month to run. Its manual counterpart costs only $6.80 a month. However, if you hate defrosting the freezer so much that you continually let the ice build up, you may not be saving that much money over the automatic defrost, because heavy frost build-up decreases efficiency and uses more electricity to maintain the same temperature.

Modern man's idea of roughing it is surviving through the night after the thermostat on his electric blanket conks out.
—*Harry Laremore*

It is important to become energy-conscious, even in our housecleaning. Here are some tips that will help you save some of those kilowatt dollars so that you can use them for a relaxing energyless vacation:

—Use the self-cleaning feature on your oven while the oven is still hot after removing a meal. You save energy by not having to reheat the oven.

—A clean oven and range cook more efficiently and save energy.

—Have gas ovens serviced regularly so that they always use fuel efficiently.

—If you own a manual-defrost freezer, don't let the ice accumulate more than ¼ inch.

—Vacuum the condenser coils in the refrigerator or freezer often to remove accumulated dust that overworks the appliances. They are located at the bottom or rear of the refrigerator.

—Approximately 15 percent of our energy bill is spent for the convenience of hot water. It doesn't need to be hotter than 120° if you don't own a dishwasher or 140° if you do.

Nothing burns up an adult's energy like a child's.
—Robert Larr

—Don't run the dishes through a dishwasher cycle after every meal. Wait until the dishwasher is full.

—Washing or rinsing dishes under running hot water can waste several gallons of water a minute. Use that wonderful energy-saving device called the stopper and fill up the sink with water.

—Wash full loads of clothes and use the water-level adjuster for small, medium, and large batches of laundry. Wash and rinse clothes in warm or cold water. With new detergents on the market, these reduced temperatures will often clean the fabrics as well as the hot water.

—Keep filters free of lint by removing the lint after each washing or drying. A clogged filter increases the operating costs.

—Do not overdry the clothes. This not only wastes energy, but it also will wrinkle and damage fabrics. Hanging clothes can be removed from the dryer slightly damp and solar drying in the great outdoors can save part of your drying costs.

—Clothes take longer to dry and they wrinkle if the dryer is overloaded.

—Irons heat faster than they cool down. Iron the fabrics which require lower temperature settings first, then work up to fabric requiring a hotter setting.

—Clean or replace furnace filters several times during the cold season. Our heating needs consume about 50 percent of our total energy bills.

Energy is important, but so is scenery. As an Ozarks philosopher once said, "Nobody ever traveled 500 miles just to look at a kilowatt."
—Bill Vaughan

---

9 Canning & Freezing

Forbidden fruit is responsible for many a bad jam.

Year after year, magazines and newspapers across the world produce beautiful, well written articles on canning and freezing. Usually there are large pictures, taken in sparkling clean kitchens, of a glowing husband and wife gleefully eyeing rows of freshly bottled and packaged fruits and vegetables as several children look on from a distance with hungry anticipation. In the interest of fair reporting, I would like to tell you how it really is during the "putting up" season and at the same time give you some hints from my mother, the professional housekeeper, on how to make your preserving experience more successful than some of mine have been. Let me start from the beginning.

I was in the middle of doing nothing in particular and enjoying it thoroughly when my mother called. "I have a friend who told me to come and get all the free apricots I want. Why don't you come out and pick some?"

Electrical impulses from the past flashed a warning sign, but it was immediately intercepted and blocked by that high-voltage word *free*. "Maybe I could use half a bushel for some jam," I said. "Golly, I haven't put up apricots since Ken and I were first married."

It was the wrong thing to say because then I had to listen to a ten-minute lecture on the versatility of the apricot. Did you know that they are starting to make gas for cars out of apricots?

Within an hour I was hanging from a tree branch stuffing yummy little orange balls into a bucket. "I've got a bushel," I sighed as I dumped the last bucket into the box. (*Hint:* Fruit and vegetables are at their best for canning

79

and freezing if they are picked early in the morning before they absorb the heat from the sun.)

That is when Mom launched the surprise attack. "Great! Now we just have to pick five bushels for Carol and then we can go home." (Carol is my sister who has six kids and lives in Pocatello, Idaho, where a lug of apricots is traded for the mortgage on your house.) "Are you sure you couldn't use another half bushel?" Mom coaxed. "They're free."

Six hours later I pulled into the driveway with gouged arms, a torn shirt, a split in my pants and three bushels of apricots. (*Hint:* Before beginning a canning or freezing project, calculate the time you have available. Do not forget to add one hour of cleaning for every three hours of preserving. Check to see how long the fruit or vegetables will stay in their prime and do not obtain more than you have time to can or freeze.)

The next morning my husband left for work early. "Have a good day, dear," he said, looking at the tons of apricots and trying unsuccessfully to hide the doubt in his voice.

"Hey, you can't leave. If the newspaper reporters come, they'll want your picture too," I answered quickly.

He wasn't convinced. (*Hint:* Try preserving on a day of the week that your husband is home to help. He will appreciate the fruit of your labors more.)

The firm ripe round edibles stared up at me, beckoning me onward. "This won't be so bad," I thought, remembering the many childhood hours I sat in a nice warm kitchen singing songs while I helped pit, peel, and slice mountains of fruit and vegetables. "If we all work together we can conquer this in a few hours and go to a matinee," I told the kids. (*Hint:* Never plan to do anything strenuous on a preserving day, such as taking six lively kids to the movies. If you finish early, take a long hot bath and read a good book.)

Rachelle, my oldest daughter, organized the stools around the sink while I dug out all the equipment. (*Hint:* Store bottles with the lids on so that they don't get so dusty and dirty. Get a head start by pulling out the equipment and washing and sterilizing the bottles the day before. Buy supplies out of season. They are cheaper and you don't have to deal with shortages during the preserving season.) By the time I unpacked the strainer, pots, pans, bottles, rings, lids, and so on, the children were in full action in the kitchen. (*Hint:* If you have a large family, let the oldest children take turns helping with the preserving and supervising the younger children. If you have small children and no one older to tend them, do your work early in the morning before they get up or late at night after they go to bed. Trading baby-sitting with a neighbor who also has small children is still a popular tradition in many communities. Of course, you can let them help, as I did. Read on to find out the result of that folly.)

Jason was throwing the fruit at Cameron, who was giggling with delight as he crawled through it, leaving a bright orange trail of goo which he squished between his fingers, extracting the pit and jamming it into his mouth. Melanie and Chris were dutifully filling the bottles with pitted apricots, worms and all. Byron had the best plan. He tore open each apricot, pitted it, separated the halves, put one in the bottle and the other in his mouth.

At noon my husband called. "I'm going to have to work late," he said.

I bit down on a pit to keep from screaming.

"Something is burning," Rachelle yelled.

I hung up the phone. Do you know that scorched apricots smell just like the turkey farms in Sanpete County, Utah? (*Hint:* If you burn a pan, fill it half full of water and add ¼ cup Spic and Span, baking soda, or dishwasher detergent. Bring it to a boil, turn off the heat, and let it stand for about an hour. Use an SOS or stainless steel pad if it is necessary and if it won't ruin the finish of the pan.)

"What's for lunch?" a little voice asked.

"Apricots," I growled.

All my little helpers disappeared in the afternoon when the temperature in the kitchen was 115 and rising. At five o'clock I was calling the neighbors to see if anybody could use some free apricots. (*Hint:* If it is at all possible, never tackle more than half a bushel of fruit or vegetables in a day. There is less mess; you can be finished before the kitchen is a sauna; and you are not so tired that you lose patience and begin screaming at everything that moves or makes a sound.)

When I finally finished the last batch of apricots, I looked around the kitchen. The table, counters, and every bowl, spoon, and cup were covered with an orange scum. (*Hint:* Try to keep the work area in a limited space. I put a sturdy table right next to the kitchen sink and cover it with an old tablecloth or old bath towels. As the juice drips off your hands the tablecloth will catch it so it won't end up on the floor. Also, it is easier to pull off the tablecloth and wash it than it is to keep this working surface clean all the time. Try to clean up as you go along. If you have a double sink, keep hot soapy water in one side. Soak the dirty dishes and pans as you finish using them and wipe off counter surfaces before the scum becomes hard and brittle.)

The top of the stove looked like a coal miner's delight. (*Hint:* That black ring around the burners that is caused by boilovers can be eliminated by covering the top of the stove with aluminum foil or by constantly wiping the area with a soapy sponge. Once a black ring is burned on, the only way to remove it is by scrubbing it with an SOS or stainless steel pad dipped in a solution of hot water with ammonia or Spic and Span added. Some of the stove stress can be eliminated by placing a deep-fryer filled with water {instead of oil} next to the work area for scalding or blanching.)

The floor was so sticky that my shoes made sucking noises when I walked across it. (*Hint:* Keep a mop and a bucket of water with 1 tablespoon of white vinegar added ready and waiting to rinse off floor spills before they get tracked through the house.) My hair was stiff from brushing it out of my eyes with juicy hands. (*Hint:* Hairnets are not glamorous, but they do keep your hair out of the food and out of your eyes.) My shirt looked like a painting by Jackson Pollock and I smelled like a jogger who had just finished the Boston marathon.

Forty pounds of sugar and twelve hours after I started this "quick little project" (nine hours of preserving and three hours of cleaning), I collapsed into a chair. (*Hint:* When giving that final cleaning to aluminum canning equipment, mineral deposits from boiling hard water can be eliminated by boiling vinegar and water in the pan. After simmering this five minutes, turn off the burner and let it soak for an hour. Be sure to wipe all the pans dry before storing. Damp pans will corrode.) Dear sweet Ken chose that moment to come bouncing in the door with the statement on his lips, "Boy, I had a rough day." He spotted the neat rows of bottled fruit. "They look great," he said, obviously impressed.

You know, there is a kind of quiet inner peace and satisfaction that makes it all worthwhile when you gaze at jars of fruit sparkling under the light. I stretched and smiled. "There's more in the freezer," I announced proudly. "And I left some fresh apricots for you in the refrigerator too."

His grin instantly turned into an unveiled cringe and suddenly I remembered why I hadn't preserved apricots since the first year we were married. "You mean that I hung on that tree . . . and Jason throwing . . . Cameron squishing . . . scrubbed all those pots, pans, bottles . . ."

Ken avoided my murderous eyes and looked helplessly at the bottles. "You know that I hate apricots." (*Hint*—and the moral of this story: can or freeze only the fruits and vegetables that you know your family likes, *even if they are free!*)

Oh, yes, that is the true story behind the delightful glossy newspaper photos, and I will never ever be trapped again! . . . Never!

I wonder if Mom knows where I can get some free peaches.

It's the weaker sex who puts the caps on jars so tight that
the stronger sex can't get them off.
—Earl Wilson

FREEZER HINTS

—Keep the freezer full. It saves energy, and when the door is open the frozen foods help maintain a safe temperature. If the freezer is partially **83** empty, fill it with milk containers of water. Leave enough space at the top of each container for ice expansion.

—Always unplug the power cord before cleaning the freezer.

—When defrosting, remove the food and pack it together in a cardboard box, then cover it with newspapers or old blankets for insulation.

—Do *not* use sharp or pointed tools to chisel the ice. My friend decided to use an ice pick and hammer to speed the defrosting process. She punctured a coil and soon white Freon gas was billowing out of the front and back doors. The neighborhood thought her house was on fire.

—Put dripper pans with hot water in the freezer to speed the defrosting process.

10 Buy, Build & Decorate the Easy-Clean Way

Progress: Our forefathers went out and built empires. Today you have to have a permit to add a room to your house.
—Grit

Many people buy, build, and/or decorate their homes without any thought as to what is easy or cheap to clean. For example, my mother had a client who put light yellow carpet throughout her entire house. Mom went there every month just to scrub that carpet and even with all her efforts it always looked dirty. In a couple of years they had to rip it out and start over.

Whenever you purchase something for your home, keep in mind that sooner or later you will have to clean it. That white velvet couch may not be practical if you have five active children or even five active grandchildren.

The following suggestions are made from the observations of two expert housecleaners. It may not be (and most probably is not) the point of view of salespeople and interior decorators.

BATHROOM

Tub: Square, round, and sunken tubs are great to look at but a pain to clean without climbing inside. The easiest to clean is still the old-fashioned rectangular tub.

Toilets: If you have a lot of boys in the house and more than one bathroom, consider installing a urinal. Anyone with boys will understand why.

Showers: Formica, tile, and ceramic are the easiest to care for. Fiberglass, marble, and simulated marble are more difficult to clean and they require a lot of extra work or they look terrible all the time. The lighter the color, the less the white hard-water stains show up. Black and dark blue are the worst colors for showing up hard-water stains.

Shower doors are more expensive than shower curtains, but by the time the curtains are replaced several times, the cost equals out. Shower doors are more effective in keeping the water inside the shower. A translucent smooth glass is better than clear glass or plastic. The latter is a showcase for fingerprints, hard-water stains, and streaking. Textured glass is hard to clean.

For fixing things around the house, nothing beats a man who's handy with a checkbook.

CARPETS

As far as cleaning goes, color is the most important factor in buying a new carpet. Even an immaculate housekeeper will not be able to keep a white or off-white carpet always looking clean and new. You can always repaint your walls but you can't always afford to replace your carpets. Yellow, orange, and light blue will also show the dirt. Never put these colors in high-traffic areas. Dark solid colors show the lint. Multicolored carpets don't show either dirt or lint.

Also watch out for carpets that show every footfall or leave vacuum marks. These usually have a short nap and a solid color. I know people who vacuum themselves out of the room and then won't let anyone walk in there for days because they have this type of carpet.

Kitchen carpets are always a debatable subject. When my son pulled out a gallon of red Kool-Aid from the refrigerator and spilled it on the kitchen floor my second thought was, "I'm sure grateful that I don't have a kitchen carpet." (I admit that my first thought was "I'm going to kill him.") If you must have a kitchen carpet, choose a medium-colored, multicolored, or patterned carpet. If a stain gets into one of these it blends in. The light colors show the dirt and the dark ones show the spills.

CEILINGS

Ceilings are never easy to clean no matter what they are covered with. Ceilings decorated with wallpaper are the most cleanable. Painted ceilings often look streaked after they are washed, but they can be repainted cheaply and easily.

If you are going to purchase acoustical tile, make sure that it is vinyl-coated, because it can be scrubbed. Nonwashable tile can be only spot-cleaned but when it becomes dirty it requires painting with a special acoustical-tile paint or cleaning by a professional (see below).

The ever popular decorative sprayed ceilings are my least favorite. Until recently there was simply no way to clean them. This used to leave only two choices: first, you could have them resprayed. There are many companies that do this and the service is quite reasonably priced. If you have damaged the ceiling by accidently scraping off some of the texture, this may be a suitable course to take.

The second choice was to remove the sprayed ceiling and texture and/or paint it. This costs about half as much as respraying, but there is a lot more work involved for you.

In some areas there is now a third choice. There is a wonderful new method which actually cleans sprayed ceilings and acoustical tile ceilings, but for right now anyway, it must be done by a professional. Because the method is so new I want to explain how it is done.

The cleaning professional first covers everything. He then uses a soft-bristle brush and carefully brushes the entire ceiling. A lot of the sparkles and loose gray matter fall, but the ceiling looks brighter just from this dusting, and the missing particles don't make a noticeable difference in the appearance of the ceiling.

Next he mixes an odorless chemical, which contains detergents and brighteners, and sprays it on the ceiling. The ceiling looks whiter and cleaner almost immediately. The chemical cleans dark smoke stains from the fireplace and black carbon stains that may shoot out across the ceiling from the cooler. The cleaner will also clean acoustical ceilings and whiten ceilings that have yellowed because of tobacco smoke.

Unfortunately, the method is so new that the biggest problem is getting the information out that it really is here and it works! Check your phone directory or classified ads to see if there is a service person for it in your area.

One humiliating thing about science is that it is gradually filling our homes with appliances that are smarter than we are.

KITCHEN

Appliances: Colors are very important to a clean look. The dark colors, such as avocado, red, brown, and the new dark-tinted glass fronts make good showcases for every little fingerprint and smudge. Light colors stay much cleaner-looking because the fingerprints don't show up. Rough finishes, such as the leather look, are pretty for a while but dirt and grime are almost impossible to remove if they are allowed to collect. Unfortunately the leather look and the dark-tinted glass are popular among manufacturers right now and it is almost impossible to purchase some appliances without them.

Buy simple! Fancy dials and gadgets are seldom used. They cost more money to buy and to repair and they are a headache to clean.

Refrigerators: Avoid buying appliances that are not easy to clean. Look for refrigerators that have easy-to-remove shelves and drawers. When I went shopping for a new refrigerator I couldn't believe how many of them have fixed shelves and drawers. When blood or milk spills in the refrigerator there is no way to conveniently clean under these parts.

Remember that automatic-defrost refrigerators use almost twice as much electricity to operate as the manual-defrost. (See chapter 8.) You may want to consider expending your own energy instead of sending the money to the power company.

Stoves:
Check for lift-up tops or lift-out burners so that it is easy to clean under the stove top. If you have small children, make sure that the knobs and buttons are behind the burners or on top of the stove instead of in front of the stove where they can easily reach them. Many manufacturers claim that the front knobs have been child-proofed, but it doesn't take some children long after watching Mom and Dad a few times to figure out that all they have to do is push in and turn. Pull-off knobs are easier to keep clean than buttons, which have to be tackled with a cotton swab.

My favorite oven is a self-cleaning oven. I have had hundreds of complaints about continuous-cleaning ovens. They seem to stop working after a few years and there is no way to clean the rough surface after that happens. Conventional ovens have to be cleaned by slave labor, but at least they can be cleaned at any time.

The glass panel on an oven door is great for checking up on how your cake is rising, but it is usually the first thing to become permanently stained, because grease gets trapped between the glass panels. If you are a peeker, then definitely buy a stove with a glass panel to save energy. If you set the timer and never look until it rings, avoid a headache and do without the glass panel. Many self-cleaning ovens do not have the glass panel and if they do, it costs a lot of extra money.

Invest in a range hood and use the fan filter system, especially when cooking greasy foods. It may cost a few electrical dollars a year, but it will save on the greasy dirt outpour into the kitchen and thus the work and money you expend in cleaning curtains, blinds, walls, and so on.

COUNTER TOPS

Dull plastic laminate sheeting (Formica), such as the butcher-block look, is more difficult to take care of than shiny Formica and it loses its beauty faster if not cleaned properly. One of the biggest problems with dull counter tops is that grease stains are hard to remove and really stick out. On shiny Formica the grease stains just blend into the shine.

If you are building or remodeling a home, consider putting a ceramic, butcher-block, or other heat-resistant section right next to the stove for hot pans. Heat will bubble Formica and burn it.

Tile counter tops are much better than Formica and last practically forever. Corian (made by Du Pont) is a miracle. It doesn't stain or scratch and it is easy to clean. Unfortunately, it is also very expensive compared to Formica. Stainless steel counter tops are difficult to keep up. They show water spots and fingerprints.

There are so many labor-saving devices on the market today that a man has to work all his life to pay for them.
—A. J. Marshall

CUPBOARDS

The darker the color on the cupboard, the harder it is to keep clean-looking, because the dark colors show all the greasy finger marks, especially around the handles. Lighter cupboards do not show up the finger marks as much. Painted cupboards are the easiest to clean and they are frequently found in the most expensive homes.

Stay away from really fancy cupboards with a lot of ornamentation. The dirt in the kitchen is always greasy and cleaning all those inset carved areas is time-consuming and tedious work.

Recessed handles are easier to keep clean than knobs because the dirt doesn't collect around the handles.

When designing your cupboards, do not leave a space between the top cupboards and the ceiling. The grease rises and settles right there and it is a very difficult area to keep clean.

Safety hint: When planning your cupboards, make sure that the area over the stove is used for items that are not appealing to kids. Each year children are burned from climbing on the stove to get cold cereal and other treats.

A bargain is something that would cost a lot more if you had any use for it.

FLOORS

Buy a medium-colored floor. A light floor shows the dirt and a dark floor shows all the footprints. A multicolored floor with a "fun" pattern will hide the dirt and scratches. Knobby or textured floors also hide scuffs and scratches, but they accumulate dirt faster and it is really hard to keep them clean. Stay away from a floor with grooves. They have to be cleaned on hands and knees with a soft brush.

Ceramic Tile: I prefer ceramic tile in the bathroom. It lasts for the life of the house. It is beautiful and easy to care for although keeping the grout clean takes extra time and effort. I prefer this to other floors in bathrooms because it doesn't peel up around the bathtub, shower, and toilet. The smell doesn't seep into the flooring around the toilet as it does in other floorings and carpets.

Inlaid Linoleum and Congoleum: These are my choice for the kitchen area. They have been on the market for a long time and they wear beautifully.

91

Vinyl: High-gloss vinyl floors keep their looks longer than low-gloss floors, but beware of claims that you will never have to wax again. Most no-wax floors loose their finish eventually. The same dealers who sell vinyl no-wax floors also sell "dressings" to restore the no-wax shine. Just remember that if you must apply a dressing every few weeks you are doing the same thing that you had to do when you were waxing. I always chuckle when I am asked, "How often should I wax my no-wax floor?"

Avoid cushioned floors. Chairs and tables may leave indentations, and even dropping plates or glasses on a cushioned floor can mar the finish. Pulling out a refrigerator can sometimes take off the top layer.

Wood: Wood floors are beautiful and last forever with good care. Some wood floors can be scrubbed with water, while others should never have water on them. Do not put nonscrubbable types in an area where spills are frequent. Many people have had sad experiences with wood floors in their kitchens and dining rooms. The movement of the dining room chairs will scratch them. If you have a wood floor in the dining room area check the chairs to see if they have a plastic or rubber tip under each leg to prevent scratching.

Flagstones: These make a beautiful entryway. They can be sealed, but sometimes this crackles and turns the grout dark after a few years.

I prefer unsealed natural stones. They collect the dirt and dust, but these can be scrubbed out with a brush. An added bonus is that flagstones never have to be waxed.

Marble: Marble is often used in entryways. It is easy to clean, but slippery when wet from the rain or snow.

Automation is a technological process that does all the work while you just sit there. When you were younger this was called "Mother."

FURNITURE

Upholstery: Decide if you want something to look at or if you really want to use your furniture. If couches and chairs are going to be sat on with children's dirty bottoms or blue jeans, buy washable fabrics such as nylon, Dacron, polyester, and Herculon. These can be cleaned at home without the help of a professional. Velvets, velveteens, and velours will spot, discolor, shrink, bleed, and/or become stiff if water is placed on them. They can be cleaned at home with a cleaning solvent, but if they become really dirty they require professional cleaning. Rayons, cottons, tapestries, and silks must be cleaned by a professional.

At our house we buy for the youngest member in the family. When I go shopping I say to myself, "If my toddler throws up on that or wipes his jammy hands on it, how am I going to react?" If I can clean up the mess without too much hassle, then I consider purchasing it.

The cleanable colors are the same as in carpeting. It is almost impossible to keep white or off-white upholstery always looking clean and new. Even upholstery with a white background will start looking gray and dirty in time, no matter how immaculate you are. Yellow, orange, and light blue will also show the dirt. One of the biggest mistakes I made was reupholstering a piano seat in light blue. I have to keep it covered with a matching towel which gets so dirty-looking from the children's practice sessions that it has to be washed weekly.

Dark solid colors show the lint but are efficient at hiding the dirt. Multicolor medium-toned patterns don't show either dirt or lint.

Purchasing furniture with removable cushions doubles its life because the cushions can be turned on the wrong side for everyday wear and on the right side for visitors.

In my opinion, buying permanent cushioned seats on a high-traffic dining room set is a mistake. Sometimes they are made of beautiful, expensive, and difficult-to-clean fabrics. The spill and splatter factor at the table quickly makes them impractical. If you have these types of cushions, cover

93

them for everyday use with a decorative hand towel or plastic protectors that are specially made for dining room chairs.

Vinyl cushions resist spills and stains, but they aren't very elegant and they usually wear out before the rest of the dining room set.

Washable tie-on cushions are just as soft as permanent cushions and they are easy to replace when they wear out.

Wood: I love real wood furniture. It is sturdy and generally easy to clean, care for, and repair. The darker the color the more it will show fingerprints and smudges. Remember that the more ornate the furniture, the more places for dust and dirt to cling to and the longer it takes to clean.

Chrome and Glass: A great modern look that is not designed for old-fashioned kids. It shows every fingerprint and dirty smudge.

Wicker and Rattan: Dirt and dust cling, but they are easy to wash and clean up beautifully.

Laminated Plastic: Wood-grained laminated plastic furniture is easier to clean than real wood, but it will never compare with the beauty of real wood. Of course, the cost will never compare with that of real wood either. Many types cannot be repaired when they are broken.

I don't know of a single foreign product that enters this country untaxed except the answer to prayer.
—Mark Twain

WALLS

Paint: Flat paint is terrible to keep clean. The dirt really sticks to it. A really glossy finish shows up all of the streaks after it is washed. The easiest to keep looking clean and beautiful is a semigloss or a satin finish.

Avoid stark white; it shows all the dirt. Dark walls show the streaks. Off-white or medium colors always keep their crisp look much longer.

Textured walls look great for a long time, but eventually the cobwebs and dirt start sticking to them and then they are really hard to clean. On a smooth wall you can use terry-cloth rags (old towels), but these will leave lint and threads all over textured walls, so use a tightly woven fabric such as flannel on these walls. It is difficult to keep textured walls from streaking and they never seem to look really clean after they are washed. The rough texture is hard on knuckles when scrubbing. It is almost easier to repaint textured walls than to wash them.

Some people go over their budgets carefully each month;
others just go over them.

Wallpaper: A good, washable wallpaper is far easier to keep clean and looks nicer for a longer period of time than a painted wall. I have had the same wallpaper in my hallway for eight years and it still looks beautiful. If that same hallway were painted I would have had to repaint it several times by now. I especially recommend wallpaper in the kitchen, bathroom, and hallways because these areas get covered with a greasy dirt and fingerprints.

Color isn't as important in wallpaper as it is to a painted surface. Of course, stark white will always show the dirt more than other colors. The dark colors do not look streaked after washing the way a painted wall does.

Textured wallpaper cleans beautifully, but I would avoid buying a flocked paper. The dust and dirt cling to it and it has to be vacuumed quite often to keep it nice-looking. Flocked paper should never have much water on it, so it has to be cleaned with a slightly damp cloth. Sometimes this isn't very effective.

Grass cloth is popular right now. It doesn't seem to hold the dirt and dust the way flocked wallpaper does. The only real complaint that I have heard about grass cloth is that the cats love it.

When buying any kind of wallpaper, check for the word "scrubbable," especially if you have small children around the house.

Windows: Storm windows (an additional window added to the inside or outside of the existing window) need to be installed in such a way that they can be popped out in sections for easy cleaning. Sealed windows should be installed on a bright sunny day. They are supposed to be cleaned well before they are installed, but often you can't see the streaks until the sun hits them and then you are left looking through the streaks for the rest of the life of the window.

The sun-screen film that is applied to windows like contact paper is a real mess. It scratches and eventually comes off if you are not careful about cleaning it. It cannot be cleaned with a squeegee or paper towels.

Window Coverings: When buying center-close drapes, get drapes that are identical twins if possible, so that they can be switched. Switching the draperies will add years to their life, because it will distribute the sun rot more evenly.

Whites show fingerprints, and the sun fades dark colors, especially dark-colored tassels and fringes. Off-white or medium colors are best.

Venetian blinds (including Levolors) are great, but a lot of people are upset about them because they are dust collectors. They are easy to clean (see pages 148–150). Dark-colored venetian blinds show up dust far worse than the lighter colored ones.

Bamboo shades are dust collectors and need to be vacuumed and washed often.

———————

We always have too much month left at the end of our money.

———————

11 The Fireplace

Wood: That remarkable material which burns so easily in a forest and with such difficulty in a fireplace.
—*Bill Vaughan*

CHIMNEY

Just a few feet from where you are sitting right now may be the dirtiest, gunkiest, blackest mess you have ever seen.

To tell you the truth, I would never have cared if a short man in a tall black top hat hadn't been in our neighborhood one day. I thought I had tried cleaning everything until I met a real-live chimney sweep, but one part of my housecleaning education was obviously lacking. I invited the chimney sweep in to inspect my chimney. He pulled out the grate, poked his head up the chimney and flipped on a powerful flashlight.

"Is that Santa Claus?" whispered my son.

Before I had time to answer, the chimney sweep said, "Come and take a look at this." Reluctantly I joined him in the fireplace. What I saw was a black furry gunk lining the whole inside of my flue. "So what?" I said. "I'm sure that anyone coming to my house isn't going to take a look up my chimney."

I want you to know that you should never say that to a chimney sweep unless you have at least fifteen minutes for a lecture. I learned that the black fuzz was a carbon deposit called creosote. The least damage it does is to reduce your fireplace's efficiency up to 15 percent. But if the creosote build-up is heavy, it could be very dangerous. It is extremely flammable and it burns with a flame so intense that it can melt mortar. Flaming balls of debris

97

can be lifted out of your chimney onto the roof, your lawn, or the next-door-neighbor's house. Smoke can back up into the home, causing smoke damage and if the conditions are right, your whole house could catch fire!

You can check your own chimney by just flashing a light up it and taking a look. If the brick looks pink you are either a great housekeeper or you never have built a fire in your fireplace or wood stove. If it is black or furry-looking, then it is time to call a chimney sweep.

The whole cleaning process took only about two hours, and watching the chimney sweep work with his vacuum and brushes was great entertainment for my kids. Now when my whole house is a total disaster it gives me comfort to know that one place is clean from top to bottom.

TRIM AND HEARTH

Most of us are concerned with cleaning the part of the fireplace that is the most visible, the trim surrounding the firebox and the hearth. These can be made out of brick, stone, masonry tile, wood, or even marble.

Brick, Stone, or Masonry: These can be cleaned using the following recipe: In a gallon of hot water mix 1 cup of ammonia, ½ cup of white vinegar, and ¼ cup of baking soda. The hearth and the area just above the firebox usually get the dirtiest. If water drips down on a really dirty area it can cause a permanent stain, so wash the dirtiest areas first, working your way to the top of the fireplace.

Smoke residue usually stains the area above the firebox. A good remedy for this problem is to fill a bucket with very hot water and have a nylon brush handy. To protect the hearth, cover it with several old bath towels. Pour Coke on the smoke stains and immediately brush the Coke out with the nylon brush soaked with hot water. Blot the fireplace dry.

If the smoke stain is really tough, you may need to purchase a brick cleaner from a hardware store or some muriatic acid from a pharmacy. These can be applied with a stiff bristle brush, following the manufacturer's recommendations. They are very strong cleaners, so I recommend that you do not keep them on hand in your house. Use *rubber gloves* and *goggles* when applying them; a spatter of either one into the eyes could be extremely serious.

Marble: Marble will scratch, so do not use any harsh scouring powders or cleaning pads on it. It can be washed with a few drops of mild dish soap in 1 gallon of warm water. Most stains can be removed with a liquid cleanser such as Soft Scrub. Heavy stains can be removed by applying a thick paste made of household cleanser such as Ajax or Comet and hot water. Spread it over the stain and let it dry thoroughly. This will take at least twenty-four hours. The paste can easily be lifted by dampening it slightly. Rinse the area and wipe dry. It is wise to protect the marble by applying a commercial sealer when it is new or after it is completely cleaned and dry.

Wood: For painted wood trim, use Lin-Sol or Murphy's Oil Soap in hot water. These commercial formulas can also be used for real wood; however, I prefer using a wood-cleaning formula made up of 2 tablespoons boiled linseed oil, 2 tablespoons turpentine, and 1 quart boiling water. Mix the linseed oil and turpentine together in a small bucket, then add the boiling water. Make sure that the bucket is disposable (such as a plastic ice cream bucket), because the smell will not come out. Wearing rubber gloves, dip a rag in the cleaner and wring it out well. Wash a two-foot section and wipe it dry before doing the next section. When the cleaner cools off, throw it out and make a new batch. Do not try to reheat it.

Greasy dirt can be removed by dipping a Scotch-Brite pad in the cleaning solution and then rubbing Lava hand soap on it. Scrub, rinse, and wipe dry.

He who believes where there is smoke there is fire hasn't tried cooking on a camping trip.

FIREBOX

There is nothing so beautiful and comfortable as a warm glowing fire on a cold winter night and nothing so ugly and obnoxious as a messy bed of ashes to clean up on a cold winter morning. There are two ways to solve this problem. First I will give you my mother's method: If you have an ash pit, remove the grate and sweep the ashes into the pit. Don't forget to empty the pit several times a year. If you haven't this convenience in your fireplace, sweep all the ashes into a pile and scoop them out, using the fireplace shovel. Place them in a large grocery bag, being sure there are no live embers in them. Ashes make a great fertilizer around trees or in the garden. Vacuum any remaining ash, using an attachment without a brush, because you don't want to stir up the dust or have to clean off the brush afterward.

Now I will tell you how I solve the problem, just by changing the way I build my fires.

The experts say that you can get the same amount of heat and burn only half as much wood by building a fire on a thick bed of ashes instead of using the traditional fire grate. The flame in a grate is pretty, but the heat literally goes right up the chimney. Glowing coals put a lot more usable heat in the room. Also, if you are planning on leaving your fire for a few hours you can cover the bed of hot coals with the ashes and the fire will still be burning brightly when you return.

So when company comes and you still have those dirty ashes in your fireplace, you don't have to apologize anymore. Just explain in an authoritative tone what you have just learned, then with all the sincerity you can muster, offer to give them a bag of ashes to start their next heat-efficient fire.

I promise that your company will go home awestruck. It will never even cross their minds that you may be just another sloppy housekeeper who hates to sweep up ashes.

FIRE-BUILDING SAFETY TIPS

1. Burn dry, seasoned wood. Do not burn green wood; it will produce excess creosote build-up and may eventually cause a chimney fire.

2. Do not burn paper products, such as your wrapping paper on Christmas morning. These will float up the flue while still burning and this could be dangerous.

3. Remember that the chemical logs purchased in the stores burn hotter than wood. Do not poke them. Sometimes they break apart and shower the room with sparks and burning debris. Always use a fire screen.

4. Do not use gasoline, lighter fluid, or kerosene to start a fire. Even the fumes can catch on fire.

5. Do not use charcoal in the fireplace. The fumes can be dangerous and even fatal.

6. Build small, hot fires. Large, roaring fires were great in the Middle Ages, but hot flames that reach through the damper can cause a chimney fire.

7. Have your chimney inspected every year by a professional chimney sweep.

By the way, the firebox does not have to be scrubbed. The heat of the fire keeps it clean, just as the heat on the burners of a stove keep those clean. If you are troubled by the soot on the walls, throw a handful of coarse salt into a hot fire, and this will eliminate some of that problem. If you do get in the scrubbing mood, do not use water on firebrick. It is made out of a porous substance that is used because it retains heat. Water may reduce the effectiveness of the firebrick. To remove ashes, just scrub the firebox with a dry bristle brush.

GLASS DOORS

Open dampers draw a lot of heat right up the chimney. This draw can be controlled by installing glass doors. The glass becomes coated with greasy dirt that can be removed by scrubbing the door with an SOS pad or a Scotch-Brite pad dipped in a cleaning solution of ¼ cup of ammonia or Spic and Span to 1 gallon of water. After the smoke stain has been removed, clean the glass with 1 tablespoon of rubbing alcohol to 1 quart of warm water. Wipe it dry with old newspapers or cotton rags.

Folks with an open fireplace say there is nothing like the first fire of the season. The second one, when you remember to open the damper, is much duller.
—*Bill Vaughan*

GRATE

Neither my mother nor I would ever clean a grate, but some people do, so here is an easy way to accomplish it. Place the grate in a large plastic garbage bag. Put a terry-cloth rag on top of the grate and pour ammonia on it. Close the bag and seal it for eight hours, then open and rinse the grate with a hose (avoid standing close).

SCREEN

The black painted metal screens can be scrubbed with a strong cleaning solution of ¼ cup of ammonia or Spic and Span to 1 gallon of warm water. Using a tightly woven cloth so that the threads don't get hooked on the screen, scrub both sides. Rinse with clear warm water and wipe dry.

Brass-plated screens can be cleaned and brightened with Worcestershire sauce. Pour it on a cloth and scrub the screen, rinse, and wipe dry.

TOOLS

Cast-iron tools can be scrubbed with an SOS or Scotch-Brite pad. For extra power, dip the cleaning pads in cleanser. Rinse and wipe them dry. To prevent rust damage, allow the tools to air-dry for at least a day before storing.

Brass-plated tools can be cleaned with Worcestershire sauce. Dip an SOS or Scotch-Brite pad in the Worcestershire sauce and scrub, rinse, and wipe dry.

12 Cleanable Collectibles

The trouble with antique shops is that their prices are so modern.
—Mildred Miller

BRASS

Dust regularly. If dust clings, rub with a damp rag and wipe dry. Brass can also be cleaned in warm water with liquid dish soap added.

Like silver, brass tarnishes. For this reason decorative pieces are sometimes given a lacquer coating. This coating should prevent tarnishing, so specialized cleaners are unnecessary and may damage the lacquer finish.

Brass pieces used for serving food cannot be lacquered, so the tarnish must be removed occasionally. I have found that a great brass polish is Worcestershire sauce. Put it directly on the brass and scrub it with an SOS pad, rinse, and wipe dry. Commercial brass cleaners can also be purchased.

CANDLES

Candlelight is not only romantic, but it saves on electricity and it can hide the possibility that you are a casual housekeeper—so burn those beautiful candles once in a while. Don't just let them sit there and look pretty forever. If you live in a hot area, store candles in a box in a cool place—the refrigerator or the freezer—rather than on the candlestick so that they won't wilt. Candles kept in the freezer will not drip.

Dripped wax on the candle can be removed (if you are that fussy) by putting the candle in the freezer and then peeling it off. Dripped wax on the candlestick can be removed in the same way, or heat it up with a hand-held hair dryer and then wipe it off. (For cleaning instructions, refer to the material from which the candlestick is made, such as pewter, copper, silver, brass, and so on in this chapter.)

CHROME

If it is really dirty, clean it with 2 tablespoons of Murphy's Oil Soap or Lin-Sol to 1 gallon of hot water. If it is only mildly dirty, clean it with 1 tablespoon of rubbing alcohol to 1 gallon of water. Wipe it dry to avoid streaking and spotting. Another method is to dip a dry rag in baking soda and polish. To brighten the chrome, put rubbing alcohol on a rag and rub it on, then wipe it dry.

COPPER

Everything said about brass also goes for copper except that unlacquered copper can be cleaned by using ketchup instead of Worcestershire sauce. Pour it on and rub with an SOS pad. A half lemon dipped in salt can also be used. Rub it on the copper and rinse. For stains, put toothpaste on a damp SOS pad and scrub.

DOILIES

Doilies are small ornamental pieces of lace that are often crocheted. They are used to protect the surfaces on which vases and other decorative pieces are placed. Hand-wash in warm water and laundry soap. Dark water spots can be removed by rubbing with Fels-Naptha soap. To shape a doily, soak in a solution of 1 cup of sugar and ½ cup of water. Spread it out on a towel to dry. When it is partially dried, shape the edges in any desirable design in the same way that you would shape the edges of a piecrust. Be patient and continue to work with it until the lace is dry.

FLOWERS

Fabric: Dust is the worst problem. Either blow it away, using a hand-held hair dryer, or suck it up, using the dust attachment on the vacuum. Use a low suction and hold the vacuum at least six inches away to avoid damage to the flowers. If the dust still sticks, each petal can be dusted by using a small, soft paint brush.

Follow the manufacturer's instructions for cleaning. Many so-called "silk" flowers are not silk at all. This tends to be an advantage, since there isn't much difference in beauty and each petal of a silk flower must be damp-dusted with a well wrung-out cloth, while washable man-made fabrics can be dunked in a solution of a few drops of mild dish soap to a gallon of lukewarm water. Rinse in a solution of 1 teaspoon of white vinegar to 1 gallon of lukewarm water. Use a hand-held hair dryer to dry them or hang them by their stems and let them drip dry.

Dried Flowers: The idea in drying flowers is to get rid of all the moisture; therefore water cannot be used to clean them. Dust them often with a hand-held hair dryer or the dusting attachment on the vacuum. Hold the vacuum at least six inches away to prevent damage to the flowers. More sturdy dried flowers can be cleaned by placing them gently in a paper bag. Pour a cup of oatmeal or cornmeal around the flower and shake the bag gently.

A good way to keep yourself from collecting too much is remembering that whatever you acquire you'll have to clean.

GLASS DECORATIONS

Crystal, hand-blown glass, milk glass, crackled glass and so on all have one thing in common—they hate kids! I have heard many people say that they never move any of their glass objects or put them out of reach when their children or grandchildren are near. They simply teach them to leave things alone. I lost a treasured hand-blown glass moose on the basis of this theory. In my opinion (which I developed with the help of four normal active boys),

105

it saves the nerves and the breakable decorations to just keep things out of reach until children get past the "touch" stage.

Dust such objects with a damp cloth. A dry cloth may scratch delicate glass and crystal. Glass decorations should be cleaned in a plastic bucket, or with a folded towel on the bottom of the sink to prevent breakage. Add a teaspoon of rubbing alcohol or a teaspoon of vinegar to the water to make the decorative glass sparkle. Do not wash in the dishwasher. This can dull and etch delicate glass and cause milk glass to yellow.

If the glass has a cloudy, hazy look (usually from hard-water lime deposits), fill it full of water and add several teaspoons of ammonia or two Efferdent Denture Tablets (this method may dull glass with ornamental trim). Let this soak overnight and clean with a bottle brush and soapy water. Glass vases that are stained can be cleaned by pouring enough cold tea or vinegar to cover the stains and let them soak for eight hours. Stains on crystal can be removed with a cloth dipped in turpentine or by rubbing with a cut lemon.

GOLD

All that glitters is not 100 percent gold. It may be gold-filled, gold-plated, gold-leafed, and so on. For this reason, do not scrub it. In time you may wear off the thin layer of gold. Dust it regularly. If the dust clings, gently rub it with a damp cloth and wipe it dry.

Gold does not tarnish like silver, but sometimes it becomes dull. Use a silver or metal polish to bring back the shine. Gilded items such as mirrors can be cleaned with beer. Pour the beer into a bowl, let it set for an hour and then dip a rag in it and lightly rub it on. Blot it dry. Supposedly you shouldn't let gold-filled or gold-plated articles come into contact with perspiration and salt. I would love to see how to do that with jewelry.

MARBLE

Dust regularly with a dry untreated dustcloth, or if the dust really clings, use a damp rag and then buff dry. Wash occasionally, using a mild liquid dish soap in warm water, rinse, and wipe dry. There are also commercial marble cleaners sold by marble dealers. Marble will resist stains better if it is sealed when it is new. A marble sealer can be purchased from the same shop.

NEEDLEWORK

I have many beautiful needlework pillows and wall hangings in my house that were given to me as gifts. All my friends know that I hate the time-consuming creative process necessary to produce these works of art, but I love their beauty and they are among my most highly valued possessions.

Needlecraft needs to be vacuumed regularly. Hold the soft brush dust attachment several inches above the needlework so that the threads will not be damaged. They can be brightened by using a solution of 1 teaspoon of white vinegar to 1 quart of lukewarm water. Dip a soft rag in the solution, wring it out so that it is almost dry and gently pat the surface. Use a clean cloth to pat it dry. If it is heavily soiled, take it to a dry cleaner.

Modern art: oodles of doodles
—Lawrence Brawn

PAINTINGS

The cleaning of valuable artwork should be left to the experts. (We have to say that because someone is sure to try to clean an original Rembrandt and then send us the destruction and reconstruction bill.) When it comes to cleaning a less expensive painting, we have plenty of advice. Dust it regularly with a soft untreated cloth, feather duster, or soft brush attachment on the vacuum. Every few months remove the painting and dust the back and the wall. Check the painting for any homesteading bugs that may damage it. Smudges on an oil painting can be cleaned with a damp rag that is so well

107

wrung out that it is almost dry. Once a year clean it with boiled linseed oil. Put a small amount on a soft cloth. Use a gentle patting motion. DO NOT SCRUB! Gently remove any excess oil with a dry, soft cloth.

If the painting is covered by glass, do not use a spray glass cleaner. Moisture from the spray can get behind the glass and damage the picture. Dip a cloth in the glass-cleaning solution, wring it out. Carefully clean the glass and wipe it dry. Use the same caution when applying a furniture polish to the frame. Never spray a picture frame because the oil may accidentally spray onto the picture. (As we have cautioned before, do not use spray polishes on real wood.) Put the furniture oil on a soft cloth and carefully rub the oil into the frame. Use a clean cloth to wipe off any excess oil.

Since we are on the subject of pictures, remember that when hanging a picture, do not use those pasted wall hangers. You may save a hole in the wall only to lose the whole picture when it falls to the floor. Use a sturdy nail or a picture hook secured by a sturdy nail. Place a piece of cellophane on the wall so that when you hammer the nail in, the wall surface doesn't chip.

PEWTER

Dust regularly using an untreated dust cloth. If the dust clings, use a damp cloth and wipe it dry. For a thorough cleaning, use a liquid dish soap in warm water, rinse, and wipe dry.

If the pewter needs polishing, purchase a good quality silver or brass cleaner. It can also be polished using a cabbage leaf, then buffed with a soft cloth.

PORCELAIN

Delightful to look at, wonderful to hold, but if you drop it your blood runs cold! Porcelain is a type of clay that is fired at high temperatures. It is fragile, so handle it carefully. When washing, do only one piece at a time and use a plastic bucket or put a folded towel in the bottom of the sink. Use a mild liquid dish soap in warm water. Never use hot water or subject it to extreme temperature changes. If it is stained, do not use anything abrasive such as an SOS pad or cleansers. The best treatment is a soft rag dipped in baking soda.

SILVER

The best way to keep silver from tarnishing is to use it. If the silver pieces are used only for decoration, the second-best way is to have them lacquered. Since this cannot be done to silver that is used to serve food, the third-best way (but it doesn't allow you to enjoy its beauty and expense) is to wrap it up in a tarnish-resistant paper, seal it in plastic wrap or store it in specially treated silver bags. There is a strip manufactured by 3M that can be placed in the drawers that will also keep tarnish away.

For everyday care, dust silver collectibles often. They can also be washed with a mild liquid dish soap such as Ivory in warm water, rinsed, and wiped dry.

Tarnish is caused by sulfur compounds in the air. There are many good silver creams on the market that will remove tarnish and bring back that beautiful silver shine—or you can be really cheap and make a paste of baking soda and water; or use white toothpaste. Rub it on with a soft cloth, rinse, and buff it until it shines. After using any of these methods, wash the silver with a mild liquid dish soap in warm water so that all the cleaner is removed. Do not wear rubber gloves when polishing silver, because rumor has it that rubber makes silver tarnish faster and leaves fingerprints that are difficult to remove. Wear plastic gloves (such as disposable surgical gloves) instead. A soft toothbrush or a Q-Tip can be used to get into crevices and design work.

13 High-Tech Equipment

COMPUTERS

In a hundred years people have really progressed. Not only do we clean and care for the cupboards, the closets, and the carpets, but now we also have to clean and care for the home computer. The experts give us some definite do's and don'ts.

Don't eat or drink above, around, or by the computer or the accessories. Coke in the computer will definitely cause damage. Don't even try to clean it if something is accidentally spilled. Take it immediately to the dealer.

Don't smoke around your computer. The yellowish or grayish tinge on beautiful furniture that accumulates from heavy smoking can be cleaned, but smoke will wear down the computer and its electrical accessories such as the disk drives or cassette player. Also, smoke can damage or destroy your program disks and tapes.

Do buy or make a dust cover. Dust has the same effect as smoke. Keeping dust out of the unit will add to its life and it will save you time because it is one less object you will have to dust.

Do protect the programs on disks or tapes by keeping them away from dust. Keep disks in their jackets. Stack them vertically, but do not stack them too tight.

Do clean the disk drive heads at least once a year. You can purchase a head-cleaning disk, or take the disk drives to the dealer.

Don't clean the disk drive heads too often, because you can wear down these delicate heads.

Don't try cleaning any part of the computer until you turn it off and unplug it.

110
Do occasionally wipe the console, using a damp lint-free cloth.

Don't ever use cleaning solvents, cleansers, or heavy detergents on your computer.

Do vacuum the monitor vents occasionally if they get dirty, using a soft brush hose attachment.

Do clean the monitor. A good way to wash it without using water (which could accidentally spill into the computer) is to use a sheet of fabric softener (such as Bounce) that has already been through the dryer. This is static-free, and static is one of the worst enemies of the computer.

It now costs more to amuse a child than it did to educate his father.
—Herbert Prochnow

VIDEO GAMES

Video games are now being combined with home computers. They should be protected and cleaned in the same way.

The game modules should be kept clean and dry. They can be dusted with a dry antistatic cloth or a sheet of fabric softener that is also treated to be antistatic. Do not touch the recessed contacts. When the humidity is low (in dry climates or during the winter when the heater is used) static electricity builds up. This can damage the game module. It is easy to alleviate this problem by just touching the module to any metal object, such as a door-knob.

Frank Lloyd Wright's definition of television: chewing gum for the eyes.

TELEVISIONS

Prevent any cleaning problems or repair disasters by never putting any liquids on top of the TV. This includes plants that need to be watered. I learned this the expensive way when I spilled a glass of water on our portable set. I immediately turned it on to see if it still worked and smoke billowed out. I was later told by the repairman that it probably would have dried without further complications if I had kept it unplugged for several days.

Before cleaning any part of the TV, unplug it! The cabinet is usually made out of plastic or wood veneer. Plastic can be cleaned with a soft cloth dipped in a solution of mild liquid dish soap and warm water. Wood cabinets should be oiled, not sprayed. If it needs a good cleaning, use Lin-Sol or Murphy's Oil Soap in hot water, following the manufacturer's instructions. There is also an excellent wood-cleaning formula found in our book *Clean Your House & Everything in It* on page 96.

The screen should be dusted often. It can be cleaned with a soft cloth dipped in rubbing alcohol, or a solution of mild dish soap and warm water, or a sheet of fabric softener that has already been through the dryer.

Television is called a medium because so little of it is either rare or well-done.
—Deane Binder

STEREOS

Cabinet: This is usually made out of plastic or wood veneer. Plastic can be cleaned with a soft cloth dipped in a solution of mild dish soap and warm water. Wood cabinets should be oiled, not sprayed. If it needs a good cleaning, use Lin-Sol or Murphy's Oil Soap in hot water, following the manufacturer's instructions.

Speakers: Fabric coverings can be vacuumed with the round brush dust attachment on the vacuum.

Record Player: Dust damages records. It is important to have a dust cover to protect the turntable stylus or needle. It is recommended that the stylus or needle be checked for wear at least once a year because if it is worn or dirty it will damage the records. Many stereo dealers will examine them without charge. The needle or stylus can be dusted with a soft brush. Do not touch it with your oily fingers. The turntable can be dusted with a soft cloth.

RECORDS

One of the problems facing your prized albums is static electricity, which draws dirt and dust to it. This gets ground into the record grooves and damages the record. So—even if you do all the right things, such as holding the record by the edges or on the label, never, heaven forbid, putting any greasy fingers on it, always keep the jacket on it, and never forget to put the turntable dust cover down while playing the records—your records will still require some cleaning.

For light cleaning they can be dusted with a commercial antistatic cloth. These can be purchased from stereo dealers. Place the record on the turntable and dust following the grooves. Never dust across the grooves, because the dust will rub off on the record instead of being picked up by the cloth.

For heavy cleaning, the records can be washed in a solution of mild liquid dish soap and room-temperature water—no warmer. Gently swish the records in the water, rinse, and gently pat dry with a soft lint-free cloth. Stand the records up in a dish drainer to finish air drying.

There are also many commercial record-cleaning products available that can be purchased from stereo dealers. The one we use in our home is the Discwasher Record Cleaning System.

TAPE RECORDERS

Again, dust plays havoc with tape recorders, so invest in a dust cover. The main cleaning problem with a tape recorder is dirty heads. The tapes shed minute metallic particles (zinc oxide) from a coating on the tape; this builds up on the heads and other parts that touch the tape. There are a variety of commercial cleaning fluids that can be purchased to clean these parts. Follow the manufacturer's instructions for your tape recorder and the cleaning fluid.

The heads will become magnetized after you use them over a period of time. They can be demagnetized by using a commercial head eraser. Refer to the manufacturer's instructions accompanying this device.

Disc Jockey: a guy who puts on airs.
—Danny Thomas

TELEPHONE

Now you can buy your own phone, which also means you are responsible for maintaining it. No more rushing back to Ma Bell for a quick exchange. Just a word of caution: you get what you pay for! We decided to buy a cheap phone for the kitchen. The first one had a defective bell. When I didn't get any calls by late afternoon I rang up my husband. "Where have you been?" he fumed. "I've been calling since this morning." We exchanged it and got a phone that went dead in the middle of the conversation—a neat trick for a dog, but not for a communication device. The third exchange phone was really exciting. When you pushed the buttons there was no telling who might answer on the other end, but it was never the people I was trying to call. The salesman assured us that ours was a unique and rare experience. We smiled as we took our refund money from him and then later placed it on a down payment for high-quality equipment.

Dust the phone with an untreated dust cloth. Clean it with a solution of mild liquid dish soap and warm water, using a well wrung out rag. If dirt or food gets trapped in the transmitter or receiver holes, carefully unscrew the outer disk with the holes (do not remove any electronic parts) and wash it in mild liquid dish soap and warm water. Gently unclog the holes with a toothpick. Dry thoroughly before replacing. You can spray these parts with disinfectant if you are germ-conscious. Use a cotton swab to clean under the dial and around buttons.

14 Pest Control

Newspaper reporting blooper: Mr. ——— visited the school yesterday and lectured on "destructive pests." A large number were present.

In this chapter you will find solutions to such problems as cleaning out the ants in the pantry and the weevils infesting the wheat, but first I want to tackle two more subtle household pests.

THE TELEPHONE

This pest doesn't care if you are talking to the neighbor across the backyard fence, cleaning the toilet, or eating dinner. Its loud bell beckons and only the brave dare to ignore it. Like bugs that have become stronger because of their exposure to DDT, the phone system has developed a stronger strain of equipment to needle and annoy you.

Call-forwarding is first on my extermination list. This so-called "service" lets you transfer your incoming calls to any telephone number. One night I invited guests for dinner and spent the entire evening playing answering service to their incoming calls. They left about midnight, but forgot to unhook the call-forwarding. At 6:00 A.M. we were awakened by "Is Bill there?"

"No!" my husband growled. "Bill is asleep!"

Call-waiting is an invention that allows ordinary people to be on equal status with doctors, insurance companies, government agencies, and so on. Now you can put your friends on hold just by depressing the switch cradle so that you can answer an incoming call. Ignoring the buzzing signal that indicates there is a call waiting is as difficult as ignoring a three-year-old sitting under your feet and screaming, "I'm hungry." The first day this pest entered my life I went from one buzz to another all day long. At the end of the day I realized that not once had the phone been on its cradle.

I will admit that the phone has certain cleaning advantages. I clean the kitchen with a different friend every morning while exchanging the latest news and swapping child-rearing techniques. I also like to fold socks, iron and mend while talking on the phone. But there have to be some rules to control this pest before it overruns your life.

1. You do not need to answer your phone if you do not feel like it. If you feel guilty about letting it ring, then take it off its cradle for a while.

2. Use call-forwarding only if you are expecting an important telephone call. Do not forward calls when visiting with friends.

3. Do not put friends on hold or jump up to answer the phone when visiting with friends. The people you are talking with at the moment are more important than those who are trying to interrupt.

DOORBELL

Like many other mothers, I have hammered into the heads of my pre-school children "Do not answer the doorbell."

One morning I had just gotten under a hot shower when I heard a man's voice in the living room. I threw a towel over my head, pulled on my bathrobe and ran out to be greeted by a deliveryman. After the man was gone I scolded my son. "I told you not to answer the doorbell. That man was a stranger and he could have hurt you."

My son looked at me innocently. "But that wasn't a stranger, Mommy. That was the truck driver."

Doorbells cannot be exterminated, but like telephones they are pests that need to be controlled. Just remember that the ding-dong is not King Gong. You are in control and you can answer it or not answer its call as you wish.

GETTING THE BUGS OUT

Controlling the insect population often falls under the direction of the person who finds them, and generally the lucky person is the housekeeper in the family, because he or she is the one pulling out furniture and cleaning the closets and cupboards. I didn't get into my first bug battle until I had children. As my babies toddled around leaving a trail of cookie and cracker crumbs, our house soon became the fast-food restaurant of the insect world. When I saw a swarm of hungry ants under the crib one morning I decided that a new house rule was in order: all food stays in the kitchen.

Prevention is the best way to conquer the household pest problem. Some practical hints:

—Clean up spills as soon as they occur.

—Make sure that all food is covered with tight lids.

—Never leave food sitting on the counter or tabletop.

—Food shelves need to be cleaned out every three months or more often if you have problems with such food-eating insects as flies, ants, cockroaches, or weevils. Throw out food that has been infested, scrub the shelves with a strong detergent solution (I prefer using green Palmolive soap for this purpose) and spray the shelves with a surface insecticide.

—Do not use contact paper to line shelves. Bugs love to crawl under its dark protective blanket and lay their eggs. Contact paper is very difficult to strip.

—Clean out garbage cans regularly. Make sure they have tight-fitting lids or use heavy-duty garbage cans.

—Clean up weeds, litter, leaves, bricks, rocks, animal droppings, and so on from the outside of the house. Keep the compost pile far away from the house. It's heaven on earth for bugs.

118   —Seal up any cracks or holes that could hide insects or let them enter.

Check window screens and doors to make sure that they fit tightly. Many insects just walk in like invited guests through these open areas.

—Carefully inspect any secondhand furniture, clothes, books, and so on that come into your house. Many a lively creature is invited in this way.

—Vacuum baseboards and corners. Clean out storage areas, basements, and closets. Pick up the heating and cooling registers and vacuum down as far as possible with the crevice tool (long, thin attachment).

INSECTICIDES

I could give you a long lecture on such exotic names as lindane, diazinon, Malathion, pyrethrin, chlordane, and so on, but what you really need to remember is that there are basically two different types of bug sprays: 1. *Airborne* sprays kill flying insects. These sprays are effective only as long as they are in the air and they will kill only the insects that they come in direct contact with. If crawling insects are hit with the spray it will also kill them. 2. *Surface* sprays kill crawling insects. These leave a thin layer of insecticide on a surface that will last for several weeks and kill any insects that crawl over it during that time.

Read the label on the can to determine if that chemical mixture will kill your particular pest, or go to your local home and garden center and talk to a qualified nurseryperson. They can give you the best advice on which insecticide has had good results in your area.

All insecticides are poisonous and they need to be used with extreme caution!! Read *all* the instructions on the can. When using them, keep your children and pets away from the area for at least an hour; cover all food, dishes, and eating utensils before spraying; use rubber gloves and a disposable face mask. After you are through spraying, wash your hands immediately several times; keep insecticides in a high locked cupboard far away from the reach of children and pets; always keep them in labeled bottles; and do not put leftovers in a smaller container or reuse the original container for anything else.

119

Listed below are some of the most common household bugs.

Ants: Ants are found in every place in the world except the North and South poles, but there is no greater concentration of ants than under the kitchen table where Junior dropped his peanut-butter-and-honey sandwich. If possible, find the ant nest by following the trail of moving cookie crumbs. Spray the nest, the trail, and the exit and entrance points with a surface spray insecticide. Caulk any cracks that are providing the ants with an open-door policy.

If you don't know where the ant nest is, you will have to go on an all-out campaign, spraying the house foundation, windows, doorways, baseboards, cracks between toilets and bathtubs, cabinets, under heavy appliances, beds, dressers, and so on.

Bedbugs: These little creatures that look like flat brown or black spots can be carried into your very clean house by used items such as mattresses, bedding, books, or furniture. They can also be walked through the front door by any member of your family who has sat in an infested train or bus. They smell bad and their bite is not only annoying, but it itches.

Once they get inside the mattress, it may be easier to replace it. The outside and crevices of a mattress can be sprayed, but do not use it again until it has completely dried. Using a surface insecticide, spray the bed frame, springs, floor, wall cracks (then caulk them), baseboards, and any suspected infested furniture or books. If the bedbugs return, call in a professional exterminator.

Book Lice: These are tiny, transparent insects that thrive in places with high humidity. They are nocturnal creatures that love to munch on book bindings, starched clothing, linens, and wallpaper. Spray infested areas with surface insecticide. Spray heavy cardboard or paper with the surface insecticide and place in infested drawers. Wash clothing and linens in hot water. Ventilate the infested area.

Carpet Beetles: These are little oval bugs with brown legs and a black body. Their larvae feast on upholstery, carpets, drapes, clothing, and other items made from animals, such as furs, wool, silk, hair, feather or down pillows, and mohair. Since all of these items are generally expensive, you could say that this bug discriminates in favor of the rich man.

The best attack against these bugs is cleanliness, because they love dust and dirt. Vacuum and spray all sides of your drapes, rugs, carpets, and upholstery often. Do not forget the undersides of drawers, the backs of dressers, corners of the closets, and the closet rods. Dry clean items that are infested. For future protection, hang the infested items outside and spray them with a nonstaining surface spray.

Centipedes: These thrive in damp areas. They really are harmless to food and furnishings and they are often beneficial in that they kill other more obnoxious pests. You can just stomp on them or commit total massacre with a surface spray.

Cockroaches: In some areas, if you suddenly flip on the lights at night the floor looks as if it is moving as hundreds of little brown or yellowish bugs run for cover. Cockroaches just love to eat and they are not particular about their food. Garbage, books, wallpaper, starched fabrics, papers, or your groceries under the sink are all fair game. They are tough little creatures that love dark, damp, warm places. There are a variety of roach traps and sprays to control these bugs. Keep your cupboards and floors clean, especially under the sink area. Food should be sealed in containers and garbage should be tightly covered. If necessary, call for the professionals, because these bugs have been known to carry diseases and contaminate food.

Crickets: I love to hear the crickets chirp at night out in the forests and country, but unfortunately there are crickets who prefer houses to hayfields. They can damage fabric and they especially like rayon or silk. Seal and spray cracks. Spray windows, doorways, baseboards, and closets with a surface spray.

Fleas: These thrive on dogs and cats, so protect your pets and the rest of the house by purchasing flea collars for your animal crew. Sprays and powders can be purchased that are nontoxic to animals (some dogs and cats are allergic to them). Spray the animal beds and other places where they climb and sleep. Use a flea soap when giving the dog its bath.

Fruit Flies: (pomace fly or vinegar fly): The type of fruit flies we are concerned with are the ones that seem to pop out from nowhere and swarm around fruit left around the house. They are especially obnoxious during canning season and they reproduce so quickly that scientists have used them for years for heredity studies. Since the maggots breed in decaying fruit, discard it immediately. If possible keep fruit refrigerated. Wash it thoroughly before eating. Infested areas can be treated with an airborne spray that is nontoxic to people and pets.

Houseflies: If the problem isn't too great, just buy a fly swatter and learn to use it. Houseflies breed in garbage cans, pet droppings, baby's diaper pail, disposable diapers, and compost piles. They are attracted to open food. Make sure all garbage cans have tight-fitting lids. If you have a garbage Disposall, use it. Make sure that window screens and door screens are free of holes and fit tightly. Use a surface spray for areas where flies alight, such as window screens and window seals. An airborne spray will kill flies on contact. Flypaper or pest strips can be hung for added protection. Observe all the precautions listed on these convenience products. Some should not be hung where food is prepared or where people sleep.

Mosquito: the original skin diver
—Robert Larr

Mosquitoes: Make sure the window and door screens fit tightly. Kill them with an airborne spray. Eliminate stagnant water in vases and pots in the house or garden. These are breeding grounds.

Moths: Moths enjoy the same delicacies as the carpet beetles and are exterminated in the same way. Remember that mothballs or crystals need to be hung high above the closet so the vapors can fall on the clothes below. When taking furs and other clothes out of mothball storage be sure to have them dry cleaned before wearing them. The unpleasant smell often clings to the clothes and furs.

Silverfish: These are fish-shaped insects that live in damp places such as basements. They enjoy the same treats as book lice and so are given the same treatment.

Spiders: Brush away the cobwebs on the ceiling and floor by throwing a damp towel over the end of a broom. Crush the spider and the egg sacs. Treat areas with a surface spray, but do not spray spiders directly overhead or they may end up in your hair. This will be an unpleasant experience if the spider is harmless, or a dangerous experience if it happens to be a black widow or brown recluse. Both have bites that are poisonous. To prevent spider infestation, clean up the area around your house, especially such great hiding places as trash, old bricks, rocks, and wood piles. (Wear gloves, preferably leather, as a precaution.) Spray basement windows and corners, dark corners in the garage, under lawn furniture, and other areas of infestation.

Termites: Never fool around with termites. If you even suspect that you have termites or if the neighbors report that they have termites, call in an expert immediately. Termites can do thousands of dollars' worth of damage to anything that is made of wood in your house, including the wooden frame and beams that hold the house together. The house will not fall down the same day or even the day after you first spot termites, so take a little time to check into extermination. Talk with several reputable companies and have each assess the damage and give you a bid.

To check for termites, inspect the walls inside and out for little earth tunnels. Like the tower of Babel they are built to reach to wood heaven in the beams above. In the spring or early summer certain males and females fly. These discard their translucent wings after mating, and sometimes the wings can be spotted on the ground or floor.

Ticks: These are usually walked through the door by the dog. They should be given the same treatment as fleas, except to use tick powders and sprays. The mouthparts of a tick burrow into the skin, so the tick must be forced to withdraw before removing it, or the victim may contract spotted fever (which we call Rocky Mountain spotted fever here at the base of the Rockies). See a veterinarian or a doctor for advice.

Weevils: There is something about white, wiggly wormlike creatures crawling around in the food that really squelches the appetite. You could be carrying weevils in every time you go grocery shopping. Weevils infest some foods while they are still in the fields. The female rice weevil punctures grains with its snout and lays an egg in each hole. Weevils are supposed to be controlled, but if one female escapes she will lay 200 to 400 eggs over a period of several months and it takes only one month for a weevil to reach the adult stage and be able to reproduce.

I have found weevils in brand-new packages of macaroni, wheat, cereal, rice, gelatin, flour, spices, and dry dog and cat food. Check the inside of the container before putting a product on your shelf. If you see a thin threadlike web on the inside of the lid, there are weevils. A closer look will usually turn up some whitish, legless grubs.

Food is expensive, so if you find weevils in new food, take that package of food right down to the grocery store and get your money back.

The problem can be prevented by freezing possible weevil-carrying groceries for twenty-four hours before storing them. This wipes out the weevil population. Dry dog and cat food should be stored away from other foods. Wheat can be baked to kill the weevil. Spread it in a shallow pan about 1 inch deep and place it in the oven at 150° for fifteen to twenty minutes. Leave the oven door slightly open. Carbon dioxide from dry ice will also kill weevils. Place dry ice on the bottom of the storage can. Pour in the wheat. Let it sit for thirty minutes before sealing the can with the lid.

If you already have a weevil-infested cupboard, throw away all the food that contains the weevil. Remove shelf paper and scrub the cupboard. (I prefer using 2 tablespoons of green Palmolive dish soap to 1 gallon hot water.) Treat the cupboard with a surface spray.

OTHER NASTY PESTS

Mice: Just the mention of this creature skittering across the floor makes my skin prickle. Still, it is very difficult not to think of *The Rescuers* or other animated movies about these lovable creatures when setting out traps for them. There are traps available for the truly squeamish mouseatarian that do not harm the creatures. Traps can be baited with peanut butter, grain, bacon, or just about any other food. Interestingly enough, according to the experts, their least favorite food is cheese.

Since I can't stand removing the creatures from traps, I use a dehydrating poison bait. The mouse has one last glorious meal and then returns to its nest and dies, where it crumbles to nothing without smelling up the house. Use caution in putting out poisons around pets and children. A good housecat will also help control mice.

Prevent mice from getting in the house by sealing up holes, especially those around piping.

Rats: A good housecat is smart enough to stay away from rats. They are always the bad guys in the Walt Disney flicks and I don't feel a bit sorry about the invention of rat poison. If they are a big problem, call in the professionals.

15 The Great Outdoor Cleaning Chores

If we sit tight it will soon be too cold to do that work
it was too hot to do last summer.
—Roy J. Dunlap

AWNINGS

Metal and Fiberglass: These are by far the easiest to clean. Hose the dirt and leaves off occasionally. If they need a good washing, add a few drops of dish soap in a spray-bottle hose attachment that is used to spray insecticides. Fill the spray bottle with water, attach it to the hose, and spray the awning, scrub with a long handled brush, rinse, and let it sun-dry.

Fabric: Clean the same way as metal and fiberglass awnings. For stains, scrub with a bar of Fels-Naptha soap and rinse. Mildew is often a problem. Always let fabric awnings dry thoroughly in an open position after washing, after wet storms, and before storing. Lysol will inhibit mildew growth. Spray both sides of the awning at the beginning and end of every season. If a fabric awning becomes so dirty and stained that these cleaning methods no longer work, it can be somewhat renewed with a paint made for canvas. This can be purchased from an awning dealer or paint store.

A garden is a thing of beauty and a job forever.

BARBECUES

Most of the excess grease deposits in the grill can be burned off by turning the grill to high a few minutes after cooking, but once a year the barbecue may need a good cleaning. Before you start this messy job, get well equipped with paper towels, rubber gloves, scrub brush, small wire, scraper or putty knife, hose, newspaper, two buckets—one containing hot water with ¼ cup of Spic and Span, Soilax, or ammonia added, the other with boiling water and a few drops of liquid dish soap added.

Begin by taking out all removable parts and place them on the newspaper.

Rocks: Soak in a bucket with boiling water and liquid dish soap, rinse, pat with paper towels and place on the newspaper for complete solar drying. Permanent rocks can be burned clean by turning the grill on high for fifteen minutes.

Burner: Clean with a brush dipped in hot water and detergent. Unclog holes with the wire. When barbecuing flare-ups occur, do not squirt water on the grill. This creates steam and shortens the life of the burner.

Hood, base, inside and out: Scrub with a brush (synthetic scrub pad on nonstick surface) dipped in hot water and detergent. The cruddy bottom of the grill may have to be scraped with a scraper or putty knife. Rinse with a hose, dry with paper towels or sun-dry. Spray all the inside parts with Fuller Brush's Oven Spray or Amway's Oven 'n' Grill Coating Spray to make this job less nasty the next time. Some manufacturers recommend that the bottom of the grill be lined with aluminum foil and some do not. Check your instructions. If you do line it with foil, punch holes where air openings are located at the bottom of the grill.

Grate: This is the only part of the grill that needs attention before or after each barbecue. Scrub it with hot water and strong detergent and rinse. If the grate is really cruddy, put it in a plastic garbage bag, put a terry-cloth rag over it and pour ammonia on top of the rag. Seal the bag up for several hours,

127

then rinse it off with the hose. Extra-tough spots can be removed with a stainless steel or SOS pad. When the grate is dry, spray it with Fuller Brush's oven spray or Amway's Oven 'n' Grill coating spray.

CARPET

Outdoor carpet is made to resist all types of weather. It vacuums beautifully. Spray it with the hose to remove dirt and dust.

Some people have very concrete opinions—thoroughly mixed and permanently set.

CONCRETE

In some European countries at the end of the day the shopkeepers and housewives emerge from their buildings and sweep the sidewalks and streets. This sounds like a lot of work, but actually it is a prevention measure, because it cuts down on the dirt that is tracked into the house. (It has been estimated that as much as a pound of dirt a week is brought in on the bottom of our shoes. Check your vacuum bag to see how much dirt is walked into your house!) I'm not suggesting that everyone should do this every day, but do consider occasionally sweeping the outside area around the entrance places and rinsing it off with a hose.

If the concrete needs scrubbing, use ¼ cup of Spic and Span or Soilax to 1 gallon of hot water. Scrub with a stiff patio broom. Rinse to avoid a white, filmy look, and solar-dry.

A wonderful aid is a good doormat. Put one at each entrance and then teach every member of the family to use it.

Oil: Fresh grease spills on a concrete driveway can be cleaned with kitty litter. Sprinkle enough of the litter on the concrete to cover the stain. Rub it in with the ball of your shoe or patio broom and then sweep it up.

To remove old grease, first soak it up with kitty litter, sand, or sawdust. Sweep it up and then pour enough Coke over the stain to cover it. This may take several cans. Let it soak for at least twenty minutes, but do not let it dry, then brush it out with a patio broom or scrub brush. This will leave a gray stain that can be whitened by scrubbing the concrete with a solution of 1 cup of laundry detergent and 1 cup of chlorine bleach in 1 gallon of hot water.

Prevent grease stains by cutting down a cardboard box and placing it under the leaky portion of the motor section whenever the car or other offender is standing in the driveway.

Hint: During the winter many people use salt on their driveways and walks to melt snow and ice. This damages the edges of the lawns and shrubs. A fertilizer such as ammonium sulfate or ammonium nitrate will melt the snow and ice just as effectively and it will make the lawn green and the shrubs grow.

OUTDOOR FURNITURE

All outdoor furniture should be protected from the natural elements (sun, rain, birds, and so on) either by placing it under a roofed patio or by covering it with sheets of plastic when it is not in use. Outdoor furniture will wear longer if it is stored indoors during the cold, wet season.

Aluminum: To remove dirt and dust, hose it down and let it solar-dry. For heavier cleaning, wash with a terry-cloth rag dipped in a solution of Lin-Sol, Murphy's Oil Soap, or a few drops of liquid dish soap and 1 gallon hot water. To restore the shine, scrub with a rag dipped in baking powder, rinse, and solar-dry. Oxidation must be removed with an aluminum cleaner (do not use an aluminum cleaner on painted aluminum). To protect the surface, apply a coating of car wax.

Canvas: To remove dirt and dust, hose canvas furniture down and let it solar-dry. For heavier cleaning, wash with a solution of 2 tablespoons of liquid laundry detergent such as Era or Wisk to 1 gallon of hot water, rinse and sun-dry. Stains can be removed with a bar of Fels-Naptha soap. When cleaning no longer restores its look, paint with a canvas paint.

Polypropylene: Polypropylene is a fancy word for plastic used for the webbed lawn furniture that is rapidly deteriorating in your yard. Hose it down and sun-dry. If it needs scrubbing, use a terry-cloth rag dipped in Lin-Sol, Murphy's Oil Soap, or a few drops of liquid dish soap in 1 gallon of hot water, rinse, and solar-dry.

Vinyl: Do not soak vinyl cushions. If the water gets into the padding they will mildew. Wash with a terry-cloth rag dipped in Lin-Sol, Murphy's Oil Soap, or a few drops of liquid dish soap in 1 gallon of hot water and solar-dry.

Putting something away for a rainy day requires a whole lot longer stretch of dry weather than it used to.
—Jack Wasserman

Wicker and Rattan: To remove dirt and dust and to keep the fibers soft, hose it down and let it air-dry in the shade. Direct sun is harmful to wicker and rattan. For heavier cleaning, use a soft scrub brush dipped in a solution of 2 tablespoons of Lin-Sol or Murphy's Oil Soap and 1 gallon of hot water. Rinse and air-dry in the shade.

Wood: *Do not* hose down wood furniture. Remove dust and dirt with a damp rag and wipe it dry. For heavier cleaning, scrub with a terry-cloth rag dipped in a solution of 2 tablespoons of Murphy's Oil Soap or Lin-Sol or a few drops of liquid dish soap in 1 gallon of hot water and wipe it dry.

Wrought Iron: To remove dust and dirt, hose it down and then wipe it dry. For heavier cleaning, use a terry-cloth rag dipped in a solution of a few drops of liquid dish soap in 1 gallon of hot water. Rinse and wipe dry. Wrought iron should resist rusting for years. Rust can be removed by using

Zud. This is a strong abrasive powder that can be found in most grocery and hardware stores. After rust is removed, paint with a rust-inhibiting paint purchased at a hardware or paint store. These paints are available in easy-to-use spray cans.

GARBAGE CANS

Rinse out with the hose. If they need a good scrubbing, use ¼ cup ammonia in a gallon of hot water. The smell of the ammonia helps keep the dogs away. A toilet brush kept especially for this job is useful. Almost all the problem of smelly, dirty cans can be avoided by lining them with large plastic garbage bags.

Put a Cling-Free or Bounce underneath the bags to give the cans a good smell.

HOUSE EXTERIOR

Brick, siding, shutters, and so on should require little care. (Around my house they *get* very little care!) Dirt and dust can be removed just by hosing them down. If they need a good washing, add a few drops of liquid dish soap in a spray-bottle hose attachment that is used to spray insecticides. Fill the spray bottle with water, attach it to the hose, and spray. Scrub with a long-handled brush or your mop, rinse, and let it solar-dry.

Wife to husband: "Look, John, the first garden tools are peeping their heads above the snow."

OUTDOOR TOOLS

Rinse off dirt and mud with a hose and dry with a soft cloth. For heavier cleaning, wet the surface of the tool, sprinkle baking powder on it and scour **131** with an SOS pad. If you prefer to dry-clean your tools, plunge them in the sand pile before putting them away. If you don't have a sand pile, put a large bucket of sand or kitty litter in the tool shed.

In humid areas it is important to coat tools with oil periodically to prevent rust. This can be done by just wiping them with a lubricating oil. If you choose to use the dry-clean method, then save a step by dumping a pint of motor oil in the bucket of sand or kitty litter. The tools will be cleaned and oiled each time. Rust can be removed with Zud. Wet the spot and sprinkle Zud on it. Allow several minutes for it to work, then scour with steel wool. Rust can also be removed by scrubbing with steel wool dipped in oil.

Handles: Wood handles should be treated once a year with any good liquid furniture oil. I prefer lemon oil. Squirt it on the handle, rub it in with a soft cloth and wipe it dry.

Plastic handles require little care. Just rinse them off. For heavier cleaning, dip a wet rag in baking soda and scrub, rinse, and wipe dry.

Hint: Grass won't stick to your lawn mower if you spray it with a vegetable oil such as Pam after cleaning.

If plants grow when they are talked to, I want to catch whoever has been sneaking over my fence and chatting with my weeds.

WINDOWS

Hard-water marks on outside windows are not caused by the rain (which usually falls the same day we wash the windows). Rainwater is soft, thus the phrase "rain-barrel soft." It leaves behind only dirt, which is easy to clean. The problem comes when the hose and sprinklers are turned on and accidentally hit the window. This water has gathered minerals from the earth while flowing through rivers and streams. When the water evaporates, it leaves white mineral deposits that make the window spotted or it gives it a white, filmy look.

If the windows are only mildly stained they can be scrubbed with undiluted white vinegar. For really tough problems, use Lysol Toilet Bowl Cleaner. (Yes, it really is quite safe if you don't drink it or inhale it, and if you wear rubber gloves.) Squirt it directly from the bottle onto the window, scrub with an old terry-cloth rag, and then wash the window as you normally would. *Do not use it on a hot, sunny day. It will smoke up and cause worse problems than you originally had.* (For more on window cleaning see *Clean Your House & Everything in It,* pages 108-110.)

———————

The reason a lot of people do not recognize an opportunity when they meet it is that it usually goes around wearing over-alls and looking like hard work.

———————

16 Car Cleaning

THE FAMILY CAR

My teenager says, in a tone of distress,
That I don't understand his position.
It seems that the key to his social success
Is the same one that fits the ignition.
                    —Hal Chadwick

EXTERIOR

Washing: I like to make car-washing day a family project. Even my younger children help. They love to take turns rinsing the dirt off with the hose. Of course, they aren't very accurate and sometimes they miss the car and hit the other kids; this starts a chain reaction which usually results in a water fight, but anytime work can also be fun, I'm for it.

Do not wash a car that is parked under the hot sun. The rapid temperature change can damage the hard enamel surface, and as with washing windows, the water will dry too quickly and cause streaking that is hard to remove. This may be too obvious to state, but make sure the windows are up. One time I took our car through an automatic car wash and one of the kids unrolled his window because he couldn't see anything with all of the water splashing around.

Before washing, remove any tar. This can be done by purchasing a tar-removing agent such as Du Pont Tar Remover. You can also get rid of tar by scrubbing it with a terry cloth soaked in linseed oil or by spraying it with Spray 'n Wash and wiping it away.

134

Rinse the car off to get rid of any loose dirt and dust. Pay special attention to those places you can't see, such as under the chassis, fenders, bumpers, and so on. (It is especially important during the winter season when salt and other corrosive chemicals are used on the roads to rinse the car periodically. This will help prevent rust damage.) Washing the car when it is below freezing is a real challenge. I did this last year and ended up scraping frozen bubbles off the whole darn car—a big long station wagon at that!

Modern life: My ten-year-old thinks a pony is an expensive low, foreign horse.
—Robert Sylvester

The only way that cold water from a hose can compete with the hot water from car washes is to use a lot of mild liquid dish soap. (When I say dish soap, I mean the old-fashioned kind for hand-washing dishes—not dishwasher detergent, which would probably eat the paint right off your car.) You can put the liquid dish soap in a bucket, but I like to apply it with an insecticide sprayer. Put a few drops in the sprayer, fill the rest with water and attach it to the hose. Spray the car and then scrub with a soft, clean sponge or a terry-cloth rag. Wash, starting with the top first. Rinse thoroughly. Do not let the soap bubbles dry on the car.

An SOS or Scotch-Brite pad dipped in Coke can be used on the license plates, bumpers, and lights to get rid of all the bugs. Scrub rust spots with a piece of crumpled aluminum foil. To polish the bumpers, dip a damp terry cloth in baking soda and scrub. Let the baking soda dry and then rinse and buff. After the car is dry, these areas can be sprayed with Oven 'n Grill Coating made by Amway or Fuller Brush. This will keep the bugs from sticking and make it easier to clean next time.

The next step in washing the car is very important, but it probably is the most often forgotten. Wipe your car dry! Drip-drying will cause water spotting that may damage the finish. Use a soft terry-cloth towel or a chamois. Paper towels are not recommended because they are too harsh and may dull the finish or even scratch the car.

Most accidents are caused by motorists who drive in high
while their minds are in neutral.
—Joseph Foss

Windows: As I cautioned before, do not wash a car in the hot sun. The water will evaporate too fast and leave hard-to-remove streaks, both on the painted finish and on the windows. On glass windows use 1 teaspoon of rubbing alcohol to 1 pint of water. It is easiest to put this in a spray bottle. Squirt and wipe dry. On plastic windows, use only a mild soap such as Ivory liquid dish soap in warm water and a soft cloth or chamois. Glass windows can be wiped with newspapers or paper towels. Bounty or Brawny paper towels are the most effective for this job.

Wash the windows from left to right on the inside of the window and from top to bottom on the outside. Then if they streak, you know which side the streak is on.

Fog-Free Windows: Wipe the windows with a rag dipped in glycerine (this can be purchased at a pharmacy), or purchase a commercial defogger.

Defrosting Windows: Carry a bottle of undiluted rubbing alcohol in the trunk of the car. Spray the window, and the ice will immediately melt off. This will also melt frozen locks and doors. A method to prevent frosted windows when the car isn't in use is to cover the windows with a large sheet of plastic or large plastic garbage sacks. Secure the garbage sacks to the front windshield by putting them under the windshield wipers. For the side windows, open the doors and drape them over the window, then shut the door.

Insects on Windows: If the bugs do not come off by washing with the window cleaner, dip a rag in some Coke and scrub.

Executive: A man who travels from his air-conditioned office in an air-conditioned car to his air-conditioned club to take a steam bath.
—*Gene Sherman*

Tires: An SOS pad or Scotch-Brite pad dipped in soapy water can be used on tires or hubcaps. For really stubborn spots on tires, wet the pad and dip it in cleanser. Rinse and wipe dry.

Vinyl Tops: These can be cleaned with the same mild liquid dish soap as the rest of the car. You may need a soft nylon brush to remove embedded dirt. After a vinyl top is cleaned and dried, use STP Son of a Gun! This is a commercial product that will help restore the original look of the vinyl and protect it from the sun and weather.

Decals and Stickers: The ever popular bumper decals are always a challenge to remove. Soften the glue under the decals by soaking it with a terry-cloth rag dipped in hot water. Hot air from a hand-held hair dryer will also soften the glue. Peel off as much of the decal as possible. There are two types of bumpers: chrome or electroplated plastic. On chrome bumpers you can use a cleaning solvent such as Thoro to remove any sticky residue. A solvent may damage the plastic bumper, so any remaining glue will have to be scrubbed off with an SOS pad and hot water. Decals can be removed from glass windows by carefully scraping them off with a razor blade and then removing sticky residue with a cleaning solvent. The sticky backing on decals on plastic windows should first be softened with a hand-held hair dryer or hot rag. Carefully remove the decal with a putty knife and then wash off the residue with the window cleaner. *Do not* use a cleaning solvent on plastic windows! It may damage them.

Decals on painted surfaces are difficult to remove and may damage the surfaces. Carefully peel off the paper, then gently remove the glue with lighter fluid. Do not rub too hard or you may rub the paint right off the car.

While we have most of the automobiles in the world, Russia has most of the parking space.

Waxing: The car may need a wax job to help protect it from the weather and preserve the finish. The way to tell if the previous wax has worn off is to see if the water no longer beads on the surface. Follow the manufacturer's instructions for waxing. Keep in mind that paste waxes need to be buffed, while liquid waxes generally do not need this. Buffing is an extra step that takes time. There is still a lot of controversy over which type of wax protects the exterior of the car best.

INTERIOR

Carpets: Vacuum these regularly to remove dirt that will cut the fibers and cause early wear. Clean them with a solution of ½ cup ammonia, ½ cup nonflammable cleaning solvent (Energine) in ½ gallon warm water. Be sure to open all of the windows! Scrub with old towels. Rinse with ½ cup white vinegar mixed with ½ gallon of warm water and wipe dry.

Floor Mats: To protect the carpets, use floor mats. Wash these every time the car is washed. For vinyl or rubber mats use 4 tablespoons of liquid dish soap in a gallon of hot water and scrub with a nylon scrub brush. For carpet-covered mats, follow the instructions for carpets.

The thing that separates the men from the boys is the price of auto insurance.
—Henri Saint Laurent

Washable Upholstery: Vacuum at least once every two months (more often if you have little feet and dirty seats on it). To wash, use the carpet-cleaning recipe above, but test it first on a hard-to-see area such as the side of the seat and let it dry before doing the whole job.

Vinyl Upholstery and Interior: To wash, use 3 tablespoons Lin-Sol or Murphy's Oil Soap to ½ gallon of hot water and wipe dry, or use a mild liquid dish soap in warm water. Because the interior of the car is often exposed to the sun, use a vinyl conditioner periodically to prevent drying out and cracking.

Leather Upholstery: Some luxury cars have real leather upholstery. This needs to be vacuumed and dusted often. It should never have much water on it, but for emergency cleaning use 1 teaspoon of Lin-Sol or Murphy's Oil Soap or a few drops of mild liquid dish soap in a gallon of warm water and scrub it with a slightly damp cloth. For deep cleaning, use The Tannery (Missouri Hickory Corp.) or saddle soap. Follow the directions on the containers.

Winter Hint: Keep a squirt bottle of antifreeze in the trunk. When you get stuck on an icy spot, spray the tires. You can also use your car mats to get out of icy spots. Put them in the front and back of the tires.

Lane borders lane
And you haven't much leeway,
In the land of the brave
And the home of the freeway.
—Richard Armour

Final Hint: Keep a pair of nylons in the trunk of your car in case the fan belt breaks. My mother learned this in an auto mechanics' class and she has often passed it along in lectures. She has been rewarded for this information with some funny stories about broken fan belts, but the best one happened in our own family.

My brother and his family were in the city late one night when his fan belt broke. He would go a little way, the car would heat up and so he would have to stop. As the car got hotter, so did his temper. His wife had attended one of my mother's lectures and tried to tell him about the nylon stockings. He snapped at her, so she kept quiet. After spending an hour in town trying to locate an open garage, my brother got humble enough to try the nylon trick. This not only got him home, but it got him back to a garage the next day.

17 Miscellaneous Odds & the End

Nothing attracts
The mustard from wieners
As quickly as slacks
Just back from the cleaners.
—*Hal Chadwick*

LAUNDRY TIPS

Socks: Almost every family has an unmatched-sock pile. Sometimes it is in a special drawer, or under the bed in a basket. For some reason both socks never make it into the washer at the same time or the dryer always eats just one of a pair. No one dares throw the extra away, because just as sure as it is gone the mate will turn up in the toy box, buried in the sand pile, or clinging to the inside of someone's pants leg.

In our home the unmatched-sock pile used to grow with each wash until all the socks were in it and everyone was complaining because they were out of foot warmers; then I would spend a whole afternoon going cross-eyed trying to match and mate all of those colors and sizes.

I have tried just about every solution I have read or heard about. Pinning socks together worked for a while, but the pins soon got lost and our crawlers and toddlers had an uncanny way of finding them when no one else could. There was also the problem of the pins pulling through the knit socks and leaving small holes or tears. Sock clips were too expensive for our large family and when we tried tying them together, we didn't feel they were getting really clean.

Finally my Grandma Jentzsch suggested a simple solution that has worked fairly well for our family. Instead of having only one unmatched-sock pile, we made many.

First I bought enough small plastic garbage cans so that each child had one, labeled each with a name and set it on the floor of the child's closet. (These containers could also be lined up in the laundry room if there is enough shelf space.) I then separated all the socks from the unmatched pile into the children's personal sock bins. Now the task of keeping the un-matched socks organized is easy.

Whenever socks come out of the wash without mates they go into the sock bins. Once a week the children have the responsibility of mating their own socks. It's a simple chore that can easily be done while they are watching TV. With a little supervision, even the little children can help take care of their socks and I have found that this is a great time to point out colors and teach counting.

There are two big advantages to this method: First, there are no more long sock-mating sessions for the person in charge of the laundry; second, because the children are now responsible for their own socks there is no more growling and complaining because there are no socks in the drawers.

Hint: Don't throw those old white crew socks out. They make great dust cloths. Just slip them over your hand and go to work.

Another hint: Teach all members of the family to turn their socks and other clothes right side out when they remove them and before the clothes go in the hamper. It will save time when doing the laundry.

Maybe the reason why there are so many leftover socks in the laundry is that they are constantly being mated.
—Jill C. Major

Towels and Washcloths: After socks, towels and washcloths seem to be the next biggest problem on laundry day. They are often dropped in the hamper after only one use because (heaven forbid!) someone might wipe down or wash up with a towel or washcloth that someone else has used. This is a waste of time for the person doing the laundry, energy, soap, and water—and each time the towels go through the washing and drying process the filters are full of lint and the towels become a little thinner and more worn-looking.

This problem can be alleviated by having all family members be responsible for their own towels and washcloths. Label each towel so that the owner can identify it. One way to do this is to use a permanent laundry marker and put the first initial on the laundry label, located on the corner of the towel. Hang enough racks in the bathroom so that each towel has its own residence. Finally, let your family know that the towels and washcloths will henceforth and forever be washed only on washday.

Science is immeasurably ahead of nature. For example, in the modern household the children are about the only things left that still have to be washed by hand.
—Bill Vaughan

Fading Jeans: It was so much easier when it was the style to wear faded jeans. The kids would buy a new pair, then promptly throw them in the washer with hot water and a little bleach. Back then no one would be caught dead wearing a pair of brand-new jeans. Oh well, the style will surely repeat itself and I have to admit that the new style looks better. But the old style made more sense, because even though the style has changed, the colorfastness of blue denims hasn't improved. They fade in the wash, and they also fade while you are wearing them. Take a good look at the seats on your upholstered couches and chairs. If they are a light color you may notice a bluish tint. If they are a multicolor, they will look more grayish. Every time

143

you sit down on your upholstery in blue denims, you leave part of the color behind you.

Many men and women are sending their expensive designer jeans to the professional dry cleaners, or they are using the self-service dry-cleaning equipment at the local laundromat. Dry cleaning preserves the color much longer than any cleaning process that uses water.

The dye in brand-new jeans can be set so that it lasts longer (not permanently) by using the following recipe: Before washing the jeans (or wearing them), fill the washing machine with very hot water and add 1 cup of white vinegar and ¼ cup of salt. Let this agitate a few minutes to dissolve the salt. Turn the jeans inside out and then put them in the washer. Agitate a few more minutes to be sure the jeans are saturated with the solution and soak them overnight. The next morning drain and spin out the vinegar and salt water. Fill the washer with hot water and detergent and let the jeans go through the cycle. Dry in the dryer. (This recipe will not work if jeans have been washed before.)

Each time you wash the blue jeans, turn them inside out and add ¼ cup of white vinegar to the rinse water. Wash a new pair of jeans with the old pairs. The old pairs pick up some of the color and it rejuvenates them for a while. If the denims don't have colored stitching or fancy pockets they can be dyed.

Efficiency is intelligent laziness.
—Arnold H. Glasow

Ring Around the Collar: Use a cheap shampoo to get rid of dirt on collars and sleeves. Shampoos are specially made to cut hair oil and dirt. Pour a small amount on the stained garment, rub the material together and put it in the washing machine.

Natural Bleaching: Boxed and bottled bleaches have been used for so many years that most people have forgotten or never learned about natural bleaching methods. Natural bleaching is great for getting out some stains that our modern methods won't budge. The combination of green grass and sun is a good natural bleacher for stained or grayed clothes. It's simple to do: just wet the fabric and spread it out on the grass on a nice hot day.

There is an antique baby dress on display in the birthday room of the famous Brigham Young Lion House in Salt Lake City, Utah. When the dress was found it was dirty and yellowed. The owner washed it and hung it out in the sun for several weeks until it was a beautiful crisp white and then she donated it to the Lion House. Except for the style, the dress looks brand-new.

If you happen to live in the Antarctic or another place where it snows often, you can bleach out stains naturally by putting the laundered garment, wrung dry, on a patch of snow in the sunshine. The colder the day the better. The combination of white snow, freezing, and sunshine does it.

Sheets and pillowcases benefit from this freeze-sun treatment and will smell wonderfully fresh. Just hang them outside on a clothesline or over a drying rack. They may not dry completely, but freezing does dehydrate the material so it will not take long to dry when you get the things back in the house. Be very careful not to tear the material when handling it in a stiffly frozen state.

Coats: Be sure to follow the manufacturer's instructions that are sewn in the coat. If the tag says "Dry clean only," do not try to wash it. If the instructions read "Do not dry clean," this may mean that the dry-cleaning solvent will cause the insulation in the coat to deteriorate.

This is also a good time to check for any ripped seams or holes in pockets and repair them. Remember that children's pockets could contain string, pencils, crayons, snakes, coins, spiders, and so on. Empty with care!

If the coat can be washed, first pretreat dirty spots and stains. With children's coats the entire front and sleeves may be black, in which case a commercial prewash stain remover is expensive to use. A cheap prewash treatment is Fels-Naptha, a brown bar of soap that can be found with the other soaps in the grocery store. Wet the coat and the soap, then rub the soap on the stained and dirty areas. Rub the fabric together and put it in the washing machine.

Close the zippers and make sure to push together the self-sticking tapes (Velcro), because they may damage anything they grab on to in the washing machine or dryer.

Fill the washing machine with water. Again, follow manufacturer's directions for temperature. Down-filled coats usually need to be washed in cold water, but polyester fiber-filled coats can be washed in warm water. Add the detergent and let it dissolve before dropping in the coat. Avoid twisting or wringing, which could cause damage and wrinkles.

Use a medium heat cycle ("permanent press" on most dryers) when tumble-drying. The coats can also be line-dried, but they don't fluff up as nicely. To prevent matting in a down-filled coat, put a pair of clean tennis shoes in the dryer.

If you think you have someone eating out of your hand, it's a good idea to count your fingers.
—Martin Buxbaum

Hats and Gloves: Follow the manufacturer's tag guide for washing hats and gloves. Some are not colorfast, so do not put them in the washing machine with your best white shirts. It is recommended that most hats and gloves be washed by hand, using warm water and a gentle soap, such as liquid Ivory dish soap. Machine-drying may shrink them, so it is best to pat them dry with a terry-cloth towel and let them dry on a flat surface.

Leather gloves are probably the most expensive gloves and they require more care. Add a few drops of gentle soap (not detergent!) under warm running water to create suds. Slip the gloves on your hands and wash them in the soapy water. Rinse in clear water. Run a slight stream of water inside the gloves to remove them without stretching. Pat with a terry-cloth towel and dry flat. When the gloves are almost dry, put them back on your hand and bend the fingers. This will help to reshape them and keep them from becoming stiff.

You can always spot the owner of a new puppy when you're at the supermarket. He's the one in line buying a 25-pound bag of dog food, an economy-size box of dog biscuits, and a case of rug shampoo.
—Colleen Place

CARPET AND DOGS

Remember the old saying "An ounce of prevention is worth a pound of cure"? This applies to puppy stains on the carpet. At least once a week I get a call from the owner of a new puppy. I always recommend two things: 1. Pour straight white vinegar over the stained area. 2. Buy the book *Dog Training My Way*. This was written by Barbara Woodhouse, the best-selling author of *No Bad Dogs*. She has trained thousands of dogs.

Mrs. Woodhouse explains, "The best chance of getting a clean puppy within a reasonable time is to never allow him to be free in any room when very tiny, unless you are there to watch him.

"Pop him back in his kennel when you have to go out of the room. It teaches him to lie quietly in one place, and he comes to look upon it as his very own home."

Mrs. Woodhouse suggests that for a small dog "an orange box is suitable" for a kennel and then she goes into detail on how to make the kennel cozy for the puppy.

When I first read this I thought it was cruel to keep a dog in such a confined place, but I had a brand-new puppy and after he had been running free on my brand-new carpets for a week, I was ready to try anything.

The puppy cried the first day of his confinement, but he was usually quiet thereafter. My family took him outside to his favorite spot after feedings and naps. He played with my children in the house only under close supervision.

I enjoyed that puppy stage a lot more after we started using Mrs. Woodhouse's method, because there were no more accidents. *Dog Training My Way,* next to my vacuum, was the best investment for the carpets that I ever made.

My tulips were
The first ones up.
There's nothing to it—
I've a pup.
—Beulah F. Smith

VENETIAN BLINDS

Venetian blinds are popular now. They are made up of narrow slats of plastic, wood, or metal that are held together with cords, ribbons, and so on. Some styles are covered with woven yarn. They can be adjusted for light control, which is such a boon, especially at the west windows where the sun is so bright right about dinnertime. Before this invention our choice was to have the sun in our face or no sun at all. Of course, venetian blinds can be bought in a multitude of colors and weaves to match the decor of the home and they are beautiful to look at.

Venetian blinds should be dusted at least once a month to keep greasy dirt from collecting. Vacuum woven blinds, using the soft round brush vacuum attachment. Close the blinds to make a wall-like surface. The brush attachment cleans the corners and hidden areas. Vacuum in the same direction as the slats. Don't forget to vacuum the side that can't be seen and the head rail. While you are at it, vacuum the windowsill and window track too.

Metal or plastic blinds with a smooth surface can also be vacuumed, or they can be dusted with a commercial pretreated dust cloth, such as One

Wipe. Open the blinds so they are level. For corners, put the cloth over a butter knife. An absorbent cotton glove is a handy tool for dusting. Put the thumb under the slat and the fingers on top of the slat and dust both sides at the same time.

Blinds need to be vacuumed thoroughly before washing or the dirt will build up in the corners and/or become deeply imbedded. When washing blinds while they are hanging, always put towels under them to catch drips and prevent water damage. The slats should be opened sufficiently so that each slat can be washed individually with a side-to-side motion. Corners can be maneuvered by draping a terry-cloth rag dipped in the cleaning solution over a dull knife. Always wipe blinds dry. This removes any missed dirt and prevents ugly water spotting which will eventually dull the beautiful colors in plastic or metal blinds or warp natural-wood blinds. Fabric- or yarn-covered blinds should also be rubbed as dry as possible. Wash both sides of the blinds, not just the side that shows.

Many spouses have made their own marital graves with a series of little digs.

To wash fabric- or yarn-covered blinds, use a cleaning solution of ⅛ cup of vinegar to 2 quarts of warm water. *Do not* use hot water! The terry-cloth rag must be quite damp (but not dripping wet) to do a good job. A wad of rag is more effective than a smooth, flat rag.

For wooden blinds or metal and plastic blinds that cannot be taken down from the window, use a cleaning solution of 3 tablespoons of Lin-Sol or Murphy's Oil Soap to 2 quarts of hot water. A mild liquid dish soap such as Ivory can also be used (1 teaspoon to 2 quarts of hot water) but it is not as effective as Lin-Sol or Murphy's Oil Soap, nor does it leave the beautiful shine. I have found that a cotton garden glove or a rag draped over a dull knife cleans each slat quickly and easily.

Plastic or metal blinds can be immersed in water for easy cleaning. Place **149** a towel on the bottom of the bathtub to prevent scratching, then pop the blinds out of the brackets and put them in the bathtub. Run enough hot water to cover them. Add ¼ cup of Lin-Sol or Murphy's Oil Soap or 2 teaspoons of a mild liquid dish soap such as Ivory. If the blinds are really coated with a heavy greasy dirt, the dish soap or Lin-Sol may not be able to cut it. In this case use ¼ cup of ammonia. Soak the blinds for fifteen minutes, then scrub with a terry-cloth rag or soft brush. Drain the water from the tub. Remove any caps at the end of the rails, then pick up the blind on one end and hold it at a steep angle so that the water will run out of the head and bottom rails. Drape the blinds over the curtain rod and with the blinds in a closed position rub them dry with a soft terry-cloth towel. Rehang immediately.

A child always returns to the scene of the grime.

BAKING SODA HINT

We have had plumbers call us and ask us to warn people about pouring baking soda down the drain. Apparently it sits in the plumbing and becomes as hard as cement. If you are going to pour the old box of baking soda down the drain to freshen it, follow it with two quarts of boiling water to dissolve it.

DISHWASHER HINT

Instructions for dishwashers emphatically state, *"Never use a hand dishwashing soap or laundry detergent."* A large amount could turn your kitchen into a giant bubble bath for the kids. Also, a dishwasher repairman told us that he has numerous calls because people use a small amount of dish detergent, such as Ivory, to rinse off their dishes. This creates enough bubbles to cause the pump to malfunction. Cheap dishwashing soaps can also cause this same problem, so stick with the dishwashing detergents that are recommended by the manufacturer. It's a real blow to pay $20 to $30 to have a repairman come to your home just to tell you that you have too many bubbles.

HARD-WATER HINT

One quarter cup of vinegar can be used as a substitute for dishwashing soap occasionally. How well it works depends on how hard your water is. The softer the water, the better it works. It should never be used as a permanent substitute, especially in hard-water areas. Dishwashing detergent is needed to break down the hard water curds. You may notice on your instructions for using laundry soap and dishwasher soap that it takes a lot more soap for hard water than for soft water.

Killing time is suicide on the installment plan.
—T. E. Burke

WOOD FURNITURE

People who move from wet climates into dry climates may find that their beautiful wood furniture will show signs of drying out and even cracking. To remedy this problem, make a solution of equal parts of boiled linseed oil and turpentine. Rub it into the wood furniture with a soft cloth and let the wood absorb it for a few days. Polish with a dry cloth.

MIRRORS

Hair spray on mirrors can be removed by scrubbing with an SOS pad dipped in hot water; then wash mirrors with a solution of 1 tablespoon of rubbing alcohol to 1 quart of warm water.

Index

YOUR NOTES & CLEANING RECIPES

_____

_____

_____

_____

_____

_____

_____

_____

_____

_____

_____

_____

_____

_____

_____

_____

YOUR NOTES & CLEANING RECIPES

_____

_____

_____

_____

_____

_____

_____

_____

_____

_____

_____

_____

_____

_____

YOUR NOTES & CLEANING RECIPES

_____

_____

_____

_____

_____

_____

_____

_____

_____

_____

_____

_____

_____

_____